YOUR PONY

YOUR PONY

Michael & Marilyn Clayton

PARTRIDGE PRESS

LONDON · NEW YORK · TORONTO · SYDNEY · AUCKLAND

TRANSWORLD
PUBLISHERS LTD
61-63 Uxbridge Road, London
W5 5SA

TRANSWORLD
PUBLISHERS (AUSTRALIA)
PTY LTD
15-23 Helles Avenue,
Moorebank, NSW 2170

TRANSWORLD
PUBLISHERS (NZ) LTD
Cnr Moselle and Waipareira
Aves, Henderson, Auckland

Published 1991 by Partridge
Press
a division of Transworld
Publishers Ltd
Copyright © Michael and
Marilyn Clayton 1991

The right of Michael and
Marilyn Clayton to be identified
as authors of this work has been
asserted in accordance with
sections 77 and 78 of the
Copyright Designs and Patents
Act 1988.

A catalogue record for this book
is available from the British
Library

ISBN 185225 1263

This book is sold subject to the
Standard Conditions of Sale of
Net Books and may not be
resold in the U.K. below the net
price fixed by the publishers for
the book.

All rights reserved. No part of
this publication may be
reproduced, stored in a
retrieval system, or transmitted
in any form or by any means,
electronic, mechanical,
photocopying, recording, or
otherwise, without the prior
permission of the publishers

This book is set in 11/13 pt
Baskerville by Chippendale
Type Ltd, Otley, West
Yorkshire

Printed in Great Britain
by Biddles Ltd, Kings Lynn

For Georgina

ACKNOWLEDGEMENT

Our grateful thanks to
Jane Thelwall for her help
and advice.

PICTURE CREDITS
Michael Clayton pps. 62,
73, 75, 76, 77, 78, 92, 124,
125, 127, 128, 129, 134,
135, 137, 143, 146, 153,
156–7, 175
Equestrian Services
Thorney pps. 182–3 and
212
Kit Houghton
Photography pps. 29 and
166
John Keene Studio pp. 30
Leslie Lane pp. 12
Trevor Meeks pps. 32 and
192
Stuart Newsham pps 7, 14,
34 and 191
Odhams Press Periodicals
Library pps. 23 and 24
Photonews pp. 2
Mike Roberts pp. 25
Ruth Rogers pp. 27
Mary Tarry pp. 13

Line drawings by
C. Bromley Gardner

Foreword

We hope this book will guide young riders so that they may have as much fun from their ponies as we enjoyed.

Buying and keeping ponies has become somewhat more complicated in a changing world, and we have endeavoured to provide advice which is totally relevant to modern conditions. For this reason, we have included a chapter on road safety for pony riders, since modern roads have never been more hazardous for ponies and horses. Safety is just as important as competition expertise, and we have stressed this throughout the book.

As a Pony Club parent, a keen rider, and a judge of hunter pony classes, Marilyn has contributed by far the most to this work, effectively communicating advice to children.

We hope, especially, that children will be encouraged to make the most of the marvellous native breeds of ponies which we are so fortunate to have in Britain.

Tomorrow's leading competition riders all owe so much to their ponies, and the advice they received in the first years in the saddle. But for most of us riding is no more than a recreation which we hope to enjoy in our spare time.

We wish young riders everywhere many years of rewarding fun with ponies – and later with horses. Above all, we hope they will always treat their equine partners with respect and take the trouble to learn how to care for them properly.

Advice to young riders is one of the best investments in animal welfare.

We wish you good riding, good fun – on good ponies.

Michael Clayton
Editor
Horse and Hound

YOUR PONY

Contents

INTRODUCTION 1

1. So Much Variety 4
2. Making Friends 34
3. Life Style 46
4. What's on the Menu? 58
5. Keeping Up Appearances 66
6. On the Right Tack 84
7. Looking Good 102
8. Fit for Anything 108
9. In the Saddle 124
10. Road Sense 146
11. Up and Away 150
12. Tally-ho! 158
13. Cross-country Fun 170
14. Show Time 186
15. My Way 204

APPENDICES

| A: | The Pony Club | 216 |
| B: | Useful Addresses | 218 |

INDEX 222

Introduction

Riding a pony is fun. Looking after your pony is enormous fun, but enthusiasm is not enough. You need knowledge and guidance.

Is it worth the trouble? Only you can be the judge of this, but generations of children have found pony-keeping rewarding and highly enjoyable, setting the pattern for a lifetime's understanding of horse ownership.

Our aim is to help you to make the best of your opportunity in riding and keeping your pony whether you own it, borrow it, or take an interest in one pony at your local riding school.

We endeavour to save you time, trouble and some expense.

The most important thing to remember when acquiring your first pony, whether you buy it or borrow it, is that young ponies are not suitable for inexperienced riders.

We will explain the problems involved with young ponies in more detail, but whatever sort of pony you are going to have, make sure that you can keep it properly. A healthy pony is a happy pony. It is in your interest and your safety as a rider and keeper that your pony is fed, groomed and shod properly.

It is possible to keep ponies in vastly different circumstances which involve widely ranging costs. Yet there are certain basic requirements which must be fulfilled, and before you take on the responsibility of owning a pony you must be sure you can manage these.

You may keep your pony out of doors all the year round, and this is much the cheapest way of maintaining him. However, when you are asking your pony for his utmost in competitive riding, or perhaps the hunting field, you cannot expect your pony to produce the same peaks of performance you could attain if he was kept in stables for at least part of the year.

Do not be put off owning and keeping a pony because you do not come from a horsey family. There are plenty of ways in which you can obtain the right advice and guidance in keeping your pony, but make sure you seek such advice. Do not rely on guesswork.

There is a common bond between horsemen of all ages in caring for horses and ponies and in understanding the problems to be overcome. The short cut to obtaining advice and practical help is to join the Pony Club or local riding club and we will explain how to do this, and how to get the best from your membership. (See Appendix A.)

Above all, you must want to have a pony so much that you do not mind giving up other things to put your pony first. You need to see your pony at least once a day when he is kept out at grass, and a stabled pony must have a daily routine of care.

We are assuming that you are going to look after your own pony, however, you should get help from grown-ups when needed. This includes the farrier and the vet, although hopefully your pony will seldom need the attentions of the vet for serious ailments. Two of the commonest errors made in keeping horses and ponies are neglecting the feet, and failing to control worm infestation. Make sure these problems are tackled regularly. Keep your pony's feet trimmed and re-shod at least once a month, and give your pony a worming dosage at least every eight weeks.

INTRODUCTION

We firmly advise that your pony should be regularly vaccinated against equine influenza and tetanus.

Have you got the right facilities? Are you absolutely sure? It is tempting to think a pony can be kept in the corner of a garden, on an allotment or even in a greenhouse. Alas, although these are not suitable homes for a pony, it is not unusual to find them used as such. Horse welfare societies all too often find ponies suffering deprivation, and the main cause is simply well-meaning ignorance.

You need a well-fenced paddock, with shelter and a fresh water supply. If you are keeping your pony indoors it is essential to have a properly constructed loose-box with room for feed, and a muck heap.

If you do not own these facilities it is possible in many areas to rent them, but make sure they are up to the standards which we will describe.

Buying and maintaining the right saddlery, grooming kits, rugs, bandages and stable equipment is an essential part of keeping your pony properly. Some of this you will have to acquire as soon as you have your pony, but many items of tack make excellent Christmas and birthday presents and you can advise your family and friends accordingly.

As with so many other things in life, the more you give to your pony in care and consideration the more you will receive. A good pony will be a friend, a companion and give you an invaluable start to a lifetime of enthusiasm for horsemanship.

Although you can take up riding at any age, it is far better to start young, and we are so lucky in the British Isles to have so many good opportunities, although it is true that riding on the roads is becoming increasingly dangerous.

Ponies are fun. We will help you to make sure *your* pony is fun.

1 *So Much Variety*

Most children's and teenagers' ponies are not of a definite breed, but are the result of cross breeding the native ponies with Thoroughbred and Arab. They may be the result of different breeds mixing throughout many generations.

Ponies range in height from 11 hands (11 hh.) to 14 hands 2 inches (14.2 hh.). A hand (hh.) is the official measure of a horse or pony and is equal to four inches, with the measurement being taken from the highest point of the wither down to the ground. To check the exact height of your pony you need a proper measuring stick which is T-shaped with a spirit level in the cross-bar. The cross-bar slides up and down to rest on the withers, the pony's height is then read from the upright stick. Nowadays measurements are becoming officially metric in Britain and horse and pony societies also give heights in metric measurement.

Over 14.2 hh. an equine is officially a horse, but many taller children ride horses up to 15.2 hh. which have pony temperaments, and there are nowadays plenty of competitions for young riders mounted on small horses.

When choosing your pony do not make the mistake of choosing too big an animal, thinking you will 'grow into' it. The danger is that you will find your choice will be too strong. Ideally a pony should be suitable for you to ride for about two years, perhaps three.

SO MUCH VARIETY

Generally, ponies of 12 to 12.2 hh. are ideal for children up to ten or twelve; 13 to 14 hh. from eleven to fourteen, and 14 to 15 hh. up to fourteen to sixteen years.

To be able to ride and look after your pony properly and to enjoy it to the full, you should not be 'over horsed' as indeed so many young riders are nowadays.

Britain is the land of the pony. We have nine native breeds. Children who start riding in this country are so fortunate to have the choice of such a marvellous natural asset, for British ponies are undoubtedly the best in the world. They possess true hardiness, a sturdy constitution and most have sensible temperaments.

A good type of child's small pony: alert, well balanced with a sensible outlook. He is being shown in a double bridle with a straight-cut showing saddle so his shoulder and action can be seen.

Your Pony's Age

Young ponies up to the age of seven years are still maturing and learning. They require more experienced riders and supervision.

It is not sensible to buy a young pony for a rider who has no previous knowledge of looking after or bringing on such a mount.

It can take two or three years to train an unbroken pony to the stage where it can be relied upon to work safely with a fairly inexperienced rider who may wish to take part in all Pony Club sports.

Young ponies need much more knowledge and attention. A young rider will have far more fun with an older pony which has done everything before and can be trusted. However, it is important to choose one that has not learned bad habits which can be difficult to cure.

Temperament

Your pony must be completely traffic proof, not just with cars but with motor bikes, lorries, tractors and other noisy vehicles. It is dangerous to ride a pony which is not totally safe on the roads now that they are so busy. Some ponies will shy (move suddenly and unexpectedly sideways). This is dangerous unless you are an experienced rider. Ponies can shy at something in the hedge and then dart out into the middle of the road, this can all too easily result in a collision with a vehicle whose driver will be taken completely by surprise.

Most ponies shy occasionally, but some do it much more than others. When choosing a pony you must ask whether it is traffic proof and test it on the road, with other ponies, and on its own. (See Chapter 2.)

There are two other behaviour problems to guard against: being difficult to catch when living out at grass, and refusing to go into a trailer or horsebox. Both these problems can be cured, but a pony which has been misbehaving for years is extremely difficult to improve.

Being difficult to catch need not be an impossible problem. Eventually you will learn to understand a pony's mind and know what will tempt him to come to you. Your aim must be to make him a trusting friend. With lots of helpers, it is sometimes possible to catch a pony by cornering it in a field, but we do not recommend chasing of this sort. It usually makes the pony a confirmed evader of capture.

The best solution is lots of patience and goodwill. Walk very quietly up to the pony with a bucket of feed and let him eat from the bucket while you are holding it. Do not make sudden snatches at the pony's head. Talk to him in a friendly manner. Then before the pony has finished eating, walk away from him with the bucket a few yards and stand side-on to him. Do not look him in the eye. Eventually, and it may take several attempts, he will follow you and start to eat again. Repeat the process frequently over a number of days and progress to patting his neck or scratching his head, but do not grab at him. Eventually you will get him to follow you around, and you may put your halter rope around his neck. If he shies away the minute he sees a halter, carry some binder twine in a pocket or conceal it in one hand and then when he lets you make friends slip the binder twine round his neck and use it to lead him to the gate where you have left your halter.

You can make it much easier to catch your pony by turning him out with a head collar on, but be careful to make sure this fits very closely. There is a great danger that the head collar will become caught on fencing or wire while the pony is grazing. The pony then panics, starts a tug of war and a nasty accident can result. Ponies turned out with a head collar on are at extra risk and need frequent checking; it is best not to use head collar in this way if possible. Head collars should always be made of breakable material. The nylon-manufactured ones do not break and can injure your pony if he panics.

One of our best ponies was impossible to catch at times, and so we had to make sure he was kept in a stable the night before a show or Pony Club rally or visit from the blacksmith, so that we avoided the terrible disappointment when he would not make himself available.

A pony which is difficult to load into a horsebox or trailer has probably been mishandled, or had a bad experience in the past. This can be difficult to cure although some ponies do respond to firmer, experienced handling. Bad loading ponies can be unsafe especially with heavy ramps about.

It is often said that temperament is everything. This is very true and quite simple to assess. Look at

A typical Arab head with the dished face, prominent eyes, open nostrils and flowing mane.

the pony's eye. Does it look sensible, placid, outward going and kind? Or nervous, worried, unsettled and sour? How does the pony look when confronted with something strange? Does it move quickly away, whip round, snort and tremble or hot up? Ideally it should look quietly, work out for itself what the strangeness is, and then walk sensibly past.

If the rider is to be safe, it is imperative that the pony has a good temperament. Remember though that overfed ponies tend to behave foolishly, and this can spoil their natures for a while. It is amazing how sensible they can become if their food is cut right down.

When I am judging in the show ring I often find that a high proportion of ponies are overfed and underworked. This results in bad behaviour such as pulling and bucking.

Conformation

Good conformation means the pony has a good shape and build so that he moves well, is a comfortable ride, and will stay sound with regular work.

Conformation is therefore important, and the best is one of substance with quality. If you look carefully at photographs of ponies awarded first prizes in showing classes, you will begin to understand what is considered to be the ideal shape.

First, the front end. You want to find a pony with a nicely arched neck and prominent wither. It is much easier to ride a pony which has plenty of shoulder in front of the saddle.

Beware of ponies that are too broad, as they are difficult for small legs to get round to control; or too narrow, as these usually have narrow necks and are difficult to stay on.

A pony with substance means a pony with good bone, which is measured in width below the knee. Usually a pony with good bone hereabout has enough bone elsewhere. The amount of bone horses

YOUR PONY

Holly of Spring: one of the most successful show ponies in recent years. Champion Show Pony of the Year for three consecutive years. Sired by Gem's Signet out of the dam Penhill Finola she is owned and ridden by Cathryn Cooper.

and ponies have below the knee indicates how much weight they are built to carry.

A pony with quality means a pony with a showy look, a flowing action, and 'presence', a fineness of head, and good natural balance.

You may not be keen on showing but it is always better to have a pony with as correct conformation as possible. Not only is conformation closely related to soundness, with a pony of good conformation you will also have a greater chance of success in any showing class.

It is a shame to miss competing in all the working hunter pony and family pony classes, and if you have a good pony you will find some of the showing classes worthwhile; there are a good variety of them in all horse show schedules. Young riders who do

SO MUCH VARIETY

not like showing are usually the ones with ponies of bad conformation.

Good conformation and movement means that a pony will be a well-balanced ride and strange though it may seem, it will make you feel as if you are a good rider.

No pony is perfect, and there is always some compromise, but it is sensible to have the perfect ideal in your mind's eye. You cannot learn about conformation in a short time or from just one pony. The only way to learn is to see lots of ponies and compare the different conformations.

You should know the important aspects of the subject which we include here. Take an interest in your pony's shape and compare it with others. The good horseman uses his knowledge of conformation

Noreen Grey, now aged twenty-one, this Connemara mare was a twin bought off the roadside in Ireland aged seven years. She has produced twelve foals, all winners.

YOUR PONY

to make sure he selects the most suitable mount for the task he intends it to carry out.

Speed, stamina, and jumping ability all depend on good conformation. So why not take the trouble to learn the difference between good and bad.

Conformation is a detailed subject, but here is a brief description of ideal conformation for a riding pony.

Head

The head should be in proportion to the body, and not too big and heavy or the pony will easily become

Champion Exmoor Pony: Dunkery Buzzard, an Exmoor stallion.

unbalanced, and heavy on its forehand in movement. The eye should be sensible, calm and intelligent. Wall eyes, where a lot of white is noticeable, are generally a sign of a bad tempered or nervous pony, but this is certainly not always true.

The Front

The neck should be nicely arched, and not 'U'-necked (looks as though it has been put on upside down). This ensures good head carriage and balance.

The front of the pony should be deep with a long, sloping shoulder. The shape of the shoulder determines the movement and length of stride. A loaded, heavy shoulder is ugly, and the movement will be uncomfortable. A good front is important, because it is better to ride a pony with a well-shaped wither and neck providing plenty of length of rein when the pony is bridled. Young riders feel safer and are kept back in the saddle without so much risk of falling off over the front of the saddle. If a pony's front dives away under you, and you feel as if you are sitting on a precipice, then think twice about buying it.

Forelegs

The front legs should be straight, with a short cannon bone and a pastern which is not too long and sloping. The knees should be prominent and should not be bent markedly forward or back. Feel the cannon bone, which goes down below the knee to the fetlock. This bone determines how much weight a pony can carry, and it should not look as if your pony is 'tied in' below the knee. The cannon bone should be flat, not rounded. If the legs look puffy it usually means the pony has done a good deal of work, especially on hard ground and may not be long lasting.

Hind Legs

Impulsion comes from the hind legs, and therefore

weak hind legs are a bad fault. The hocks should be large with prominent points.

When a pony is viewed from the front, or rear, the front and hind legs should appear straight. Legs or feet that turn in or out are not correct. You should get someone else to lead the pony away from you and then turn and approach you. This should be done at a walk and again at a trot. Watch carefully to see whether the pony moves straight. There are all sorts of variations from unblemished straight movement:
Brushing: if the feet are set too close together they may knock into the other leg, particularly at the fetlock, causing injury.
Cow hocks: hocks that turn in.
Dishing: a movement in which the front feet swing out sideways.
Pigeon toes: feet pointing in (although one of our best ponies had this fault).
Plaiting: a weaving movement with the front legs causing the pony to cross his legs.

Blemishes include:
Capped hocks: puffy enlargements on the point of the hock.
Curbs: enlargements below the point of the hock.
Splints: bony lumps on the cannon bones caused by jarring.

You use this trotting-up procedure to test whether the pony is sound. If it is not putting equal weight on each foot in a rhythmic way, then it is lame. It will take its weight off one leg more quickly than the others because it is hurting. You then need expert advice. Even experts can be mistaken as to which leg is the lame one unless the animal is badly lame when it will be all too obvious.

The Middle

A pony should ideally have a deep girth, with a good distance from the wither to just behind the elbow.

There is then plenty of room for the heart. The rib cage should be nicely rounded not flat-sided, so there is good room for the ribs and lungs. When seen from the front the width of the chest should be in proportion to the rest of the pony. If too narrow, then both the forelegs will appear to come out of one hole, and the heart room will be limited.

The Quarters

Good quarters should always look well-rounded and muscular with strong thighs. They should not slope too steeply from the croup to the dock to be correct for showing, although sometimes this indicates a good jumper. From behind, the quarters should look square and level across the top. If the tail is set on high, and is well carried, it will always look better than a low set one, but the appearance of a tail can always be improved by good pulling and trimming.

Feet

There is an old saying: no foot, no horse. This emphasizes the vital importance of the soundness of the feet. The feet should be a pair with wide heels, the frogs well developed, and the soles of the feet arched and not too flat. If you look at the surface they should be free from rings and grooves. The angle of slope should be the same for both feet and they should not appear small or 'boxy'. If a pony has had laminitis, when you pick up the foot you will find the soles of the foot will have dropped, and the surface will be flat. (See Chapter 8.) Flat feet soon get bruised and corns may be likely.

We have described the ideal conformation. If a pony has good conformation then it will remain sound, and be long lasting. Ponies that move badly put more strain on their joints and limbs and these wear out in time. Our native breeds are basically sound. Most of these ponies remain sound and are capable of being ridden regularly until they are well over twenty years of age.

Sexes

Adult ponies are either mares (females) or geldings (castrated or 'cut' males). Pony stallions are rarely used for riding ponies. They are kept for breeding purposes and showing. Male ponies are usually castrated as foals or yearlings.

Young ponies up to the age of four are fillies (females), or colts (males). All youngsters under one year are known as filly foals or colt foals. We refer in this book to your pony as 'he' although it equally applies to mares.

Age

The age of a pony or horse is calculated as if it was born on 1 May, however, Thoroughbred horses are dated from 1 January. So a yearling becomes a two year old on 1 May the following year, on 1 January if it is a Thoroughbred. The term 'aged' is used to describe a pony eight years or over, but it does not mean that it is old. Ponies can usually be ridden up to the age of twenty and some live to be thirty. However, it does become difficult to judge the age of some ponies in their advanced years.

A pony's age is determined by looking at its teeth. This is a little complicated, but you should have some idea of how this is done. Up to the age of six a pony loses his milk teeth as children do, and these are replaced by permanent teeth.

At seven a hook begins to appear on the top corner tooth; the teeth begin to become more slanted and the tables of the teeth become worn. At the age of thirteen a groove starts to appear at the top edge of the outside front incisor tooth which finally reaches the bottom of the tooth at nineteen. This is called Galvayne's groove after the man who first discovered how it indicated age.

SO MUCH VARIETY

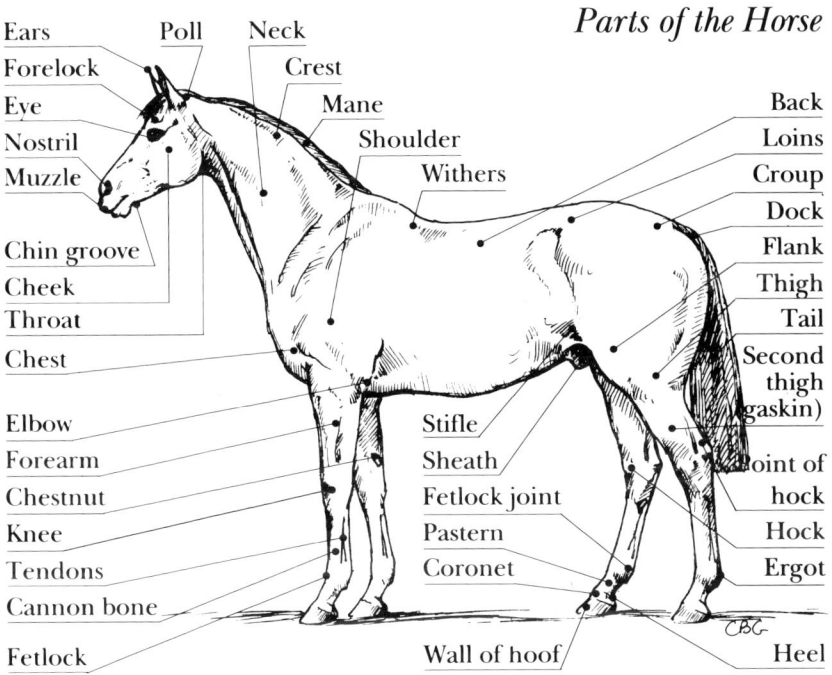

Parts of the Horse

Your vet will be able to tell the age of your pony accurately when he inspects it before you buy it.

Points Of the Horse

The parts of your pony are known as 'Points of the Horse' and are the same for horses and ponies. (See diagram.)

The near-side of the pony is the left side; the right side is the off-side.

Colours

Appaloosa: ponies with an unusual spotted coat.
Bay: brown with black mane, tail and legs (known as 'points').
Black: this is a rare colour, as most ponies have a brown muzzle so they are called brown in colour. Horses are occasionally black. The colour overall is decided by the colour of the muzzle.

Blue roan: black or dark brown hairs intermingled with white hairs to give a blue colour, with black points. Ponies of this colour are usually very tough.
Brown: dark brown all over including mane and tail.
Chestnut: varies in shade from a liver chestnut to light chestnut. A chestnut pony sometimes has a lighter coloured mane and tail (called flaxen). This colour sometimes goes with a more excitable temperament.
Dun: beige or yellow coloured with black points and often a black line running along the spine called a dorsal stripe or list.
Grey: any sort of white or grey colour from near-white to iron grey. Ponies and horses are never called white.
Palomino: golden body with blond mane and tail.
Piebald: areas of white and patches of black only.
Skewbald: patches of white with patches of brown or other colours such as roan.
Strawberry roan: chestnut and white hairs intermingled.

Markings

Blaze: a broad white band down the face.
Star: an approximately circular white mark in the centre of the forehead.
Stripe: a narrow band down the face.
Wall eye: an eye with white in it, caused by lack of pigmentation. It is not a defect of the eye. It is not a true marking, but can be used for identification purposes.
White sock: white hair from the coronet to just above the fetlock.
White stocking: white hair from the coronet to the knee.

Brand Marks

Brand marks are often seen on the native ponies

born on moorlands of New Forest, Welsh, Dartmoor and Exmoor breeding. Ponies are branded by the breeder, so that their stock can be recognized on the moors. The brands are either placed on the flat of the shoulder, the saddle or hind quarter regions.

Freeze Brands

Freeze bands are becoming widespread for security reasons. Your pony can be freeze branded with nitrous oxide, which is not painful. The brand numbers and letters show up in white on the saddle region. Greys are usually branded on the shoulder, and the brands are more difficult to see. The brand mark is registered in your ownership at a central office, and if your pony is missing or stolen you can contact the office immediately. They will then notify all the slaughter houses to check your pony is not being sold for meat.

Pony theft from fields in this country is increasing, but a pony with a good clear registration mark can be identified quickly. Details of the mark can be given to the police. It is not possible to remove the freeze mark. If you are purchasing a pony with a freeze mark you should check the rightful owner and complete a registration form as the new owner.

Freeze marking is inexpensive and lasts for your pony's life. It is sensible to get this organized for a week before you need to ride the pony, as the saddle area is slightly sensitive for a few days.

Different Types of Pony

Sometimes ponies can be used for two or more categories.
First ridden pony: a pony with good conformation and temperament suitable for children to show in their first classes off the leading rein.
Gymkhana pony: ponies schooled for gymkhana races and games. Usually Welsh and very fast.
Leading rein pony: a pony with good conformation

and temperament suitable for children up to the age of seven to show in the ring.
Polo pony: usually not a pony at all but a small horse of about 15.2 hh. used for the game of polo.
Pony Club eventer: a pony for Pony Club one or two day eventing, with dressage, cross country and show jumping. Ponies can range in height from junior classes at 12.2 up to 16 hh. or over for open classes.
Show hunter pony: a well-bred pony with quality and substance. Not so fine boned as a show pony and does not have such exaggerated action.
Show jumping pony: a pony for show jumping which can be any conformation and movement. The only requirement is jumping ability in a controlled area.
Show pony: a fine, well-bred pony with quality of conformation and movement.
Working hunter pony: a show hunter pony that is used for jumping, usually a natural course of rustic fences similar to those found out hunting.

Breeds

Anglo Arab: a cross between a Thoroughbred and Arab.
Arab: the Arab is noted for its beauty, stamina and endurance. It is also noted for its soundness. The characteristics are a refined head and graceful action. The height is from around 14.2 to 15 hh.
Native Breeds: there are nine native breeds of the British Isles which we have been lucky to inherit. These are discussed in detail later in this chapter under Our Heritage.
Thoroughbred: this means a horse registered in the General Stud Book and mainly used in racing. The Thoroughbred is fast with a highly strung temperament, and the height can range from 15 to 17 hh.

Most moorland ponies provide wonderful foundation stock when mated with Arab, Thoroughbred, or other blood. Many a good hunter contains some

SO MUCH VARIETY

pony blood somewhere in its ancestry, and a straight cross, especially with Welsh blood, still produces excellent working hunters.

There are pure Thoroughbred ponies, but they are really Thoroughbred horses which have simply failed to make 15 hh., and thus qualify as ponies for size, but may not have the pony characteristics. The leading show ponies are often produced by mating pony mares to Thoroughbred stallions, ideally giving quality plus true pony advantages of temperament and toughness in conformation. Trying to get the right balance of qualities is something of a gamble.

The Arab, the oldest and the most beautiful of all horse breeds in the world, has had an important influence in producing first-class riding ponies.

Ardencaple: one of the great influences on pony breeding, this small Thoroughbred stallion was owned by Mrs G. Spooner, a founder of Ponies of Britain. Note his quality and fine conformation.

Arab presence, carriage and toughness, can be transmitted with great value in mating Arab stallions with pony mares, but such crossing must be carefully thought out.

The Arab itself is described as a horse, although it may technically qualify as a pony in height when it is about 14.2 hh. Every English Thoroughbred has Arab blood in its ancestry, although the best modern Thoroughbred inevitably beats the Arab in speed and jumping scope. Some of the most striking show ponies contain Thoroughbred, Arab and native pony blood. The best Arabs in the world are nowadays bred in Britain.

The Palomino is not a breed, but a type in Britain, and its popularity undoubtedly depends on its

Radfan: a fine example of a young Arabian stallion, sired by Dancing King out of the dam Bint Yasimet.

SO MUCH VARIETY

'pretty' appearance: golden coat with white mane and tail – cream is not good enough – and measuring 14.2 hh.

Apart from all the specific breeds and types there is a host of others, mongrels if you like, but often possessing most of the virtues desired in our ponies. They cannot be entered in stud books, nor registered as moorland breeds, but such ponies still form the bulk of those which many of us ride or drive.

Each is individual, deserving every bit as much care and attention as his 'pure-bred' cousins. Most have a considerable amount of native blood, and thus possess the essential ability to thrive when kept out of doors.

Ponies being herded off Dartmoor at Chagford. They are not pure bred but a mixture of crossbreds. Living out on the moor helps to give them a hardy constitution.

Our Heritage

It is easy to take ponies for granted. How many children appreciate our wonderful good fortune in the British Isles? Of course ponies are found abroad, but we have a unique range of superb ponies – each type with distinct characteristics, and all with basic qualities of toughness, courage, and intelligence.

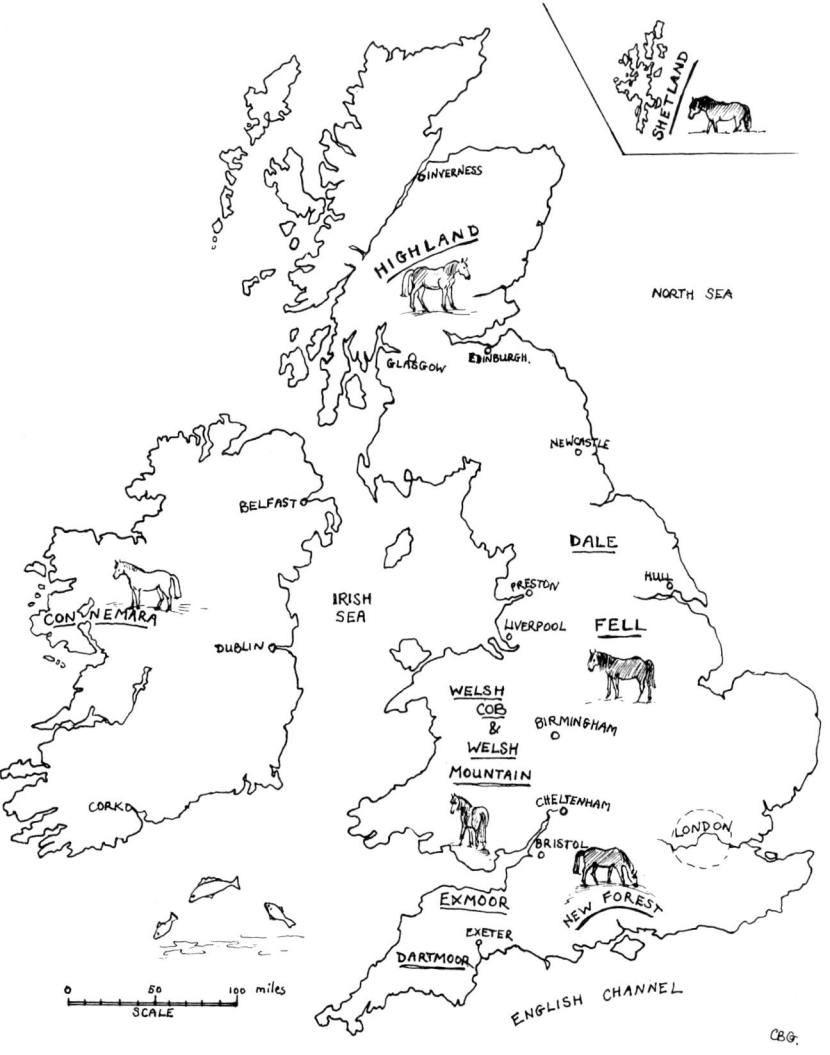

SO MUCH VARIETY

The presence of ponies in these islands is indeed a precious heritage. Some breeds have in the past been in danger of extinction through lack of interest and money, through ruthless slaughter for the meat trade, or careless cross-breeding which threatened to submerge a distinct breed.

Nowadays, the value placed on ponies has never been greater, although there are some problems of over-production. The growth of trekking holidays has been a considerable factor in helping to preserve the native breeds. There are many excellent centres providing marvellous holidays in Britain's moorlands and forests.

Connemara

Greys are numerous among them, but blacks, bays, browns, duns are found, with occasionally roans and

Connemara mare with her foal. The foal will turn grey later. This hardy Irish breed makes a marvellous riding pony and is exceptionally useful when crossed with Thoroughbred stallions to make hunters and competition horses.

25

chestnuts. They are from 13 to 14.2 hh., and can make excellent mounts for adults as well as children.

The origins of Connemara ponies, which are found above Galway Bay on the Connaught coast of Ireland, are very old. Their homeland is beautiful, but wild, and the original pony type which evolved there had to be extremely hardy.

Connemaras tend to have good temperament, and their conformation ideally includes good well-sloped shoulders, and well-balanced head and neck.

Dales

The 'dark horses' of the pony world, since they are among the largest of the pony breeds, and should be jet-black or dark bay and brown, or occasionally grey.

Dale ponies should be 14 to 14.2 hh., and while having neat, pony heads, they have strong conformation, with plenty of bone below the knee; they grow ample hair, known as 'feather' on their heels. In the nineteenth century, they carried lead from the Northumberland and Durham mines to the docks in convoys – a working background which has helped to produce ponies of great strength and hardiness.

They have gained in popularity in recent years, especially because of their usefulness as trekking ponies, since they are up to substantial weights. They are up to hard work in harness, including farm jobs such as ploughing, so they have all-round usefulness.

Dartmoor

A strong attractive pony, the Dartmoor can be seen carrying smaller adults with ease and confidence across the rugged contours of his native moorland in Devon. Herds of these ponies roam Dartmoor and breed naturally, being rounded up only for branding or sale.

SO MUCH VARIETY

Dartmoor: a Champion Dartmoor mare with her foal.

Dartmoor ponies should be no higher than 12.2 hh., preferably of bay, black, or brown, although only skewbalds and piebalds are barred from registration as Dartmoors. If they are to become children's ponies they should be handled as much as possible when young. They have nice temperaments, and have a pleasingly neat appearance. They are often used for driving.

Exmoor

Anyone who has seen shepherds riding Exmoor ponies on their native moorland in Devon and Somerset would not doubt the toughness and stamina of these ponies which should not exceed 12.2 hh. in mares, and 12.3 hh. in stallions. They are brown, bay or dun, with no white markings, and Exmoors have a characteristic mealy-coloured nose. They have a distinctive mealy colour around the eye, known on Exmoor as 'toad eye', and there is often a fan-like growth at the top of the tail, called an 'ice-tail'.

YOUR PONY

Exmoor: pure-bred Exmoor ponies in their native setting. Note their mealy mouths, one of the special characteristics of this ancient moorland breed.

Well schooled, they are excellent ponies for children, especially as working hunters, but they are not necessarily the best breed to choose as a first pony.

Fell

Coming from the west side of the Pennine Chain, the Fell pony is another animal formerly used to carry heavy packs, like his neighbours in the dales. Sometimes the loads carried could be as heavy as 16 stone, carried in two panniers slung either side of the pony's spine.

This is a useful, all-purpose breed, from 12.2 to 14 hh., often black, with some bays, browns or greys, but not broken colours, and preferably without white markings. They are powerfully built, but should have sloping well-laid-back shoulders, ideal for riding purposes, although they make driving ponies as well. They breed true to type consistently, and do well in mountain and moorland showing classes. They have quiet, no-nonsense temperaments, if properly handled.

Highland

Even if you have never seen the Highland pony in his natural environment north of the border, you must surely recall the popular picture of this famous breed, standing in a glen, with a deer slung across his back. Their history of weight-carrying in Scotland, bearing loads for crofters, bringing home the results of deer-stalking expeditions, has given Highland ponies wonderfully tough constitutions, with special value in hilly areas.

They are especially useful in the growing sport of pony trekking, offering an enjoyable method of exploring the beautiful scenery of their homeland. They make good riding ponies, with equable temperaments, and sometimes with excellent jumping capability. The pure-bred Highland pony is usually about 13 hh., and should not be above 14 hh.; there is a larger type up to 14.2 hh. The colour is generally black although dark brown and bay can be seen.

New Forest

Known to millions of holiday-makers on the South Coast because they are so easily seen from the roads in their native Hampshire home, these ponies are deservedly among the most popular. Fortunately, the two major roads through the New Forest are now largely fenced, cutting down the grievous road accidents in which ponies were so often maimed and killed, but it is a cruel act to feed these ponies on roads, since it encourages them to haunt the highways and risk accidents.

The New Forest survives as Crown land with its grassy glades, open moorland, and marshes deep within the forest. The keep for ponies is sometimes very sparse, especially in the surprisingly harsh winters which can occasionally afflict this southern coastal area.

The ponies thus have good reason for being hardy, and good 'doers'. They do flourish much

YOUR PONY

New Forest: Champion New Forest shown in hand. This hardy South of England breed still flourishes in its original Norman forest home in Hampshire but it is also bred widely in studs in Britain and abroad.

more happily on somewhat better keep than that of the forest, the youngsters tending to grow taller and stronger, yet retaining their native characteristics of toughness and sure-footedness.

New Forest ponies are from 12 to 14.2 hh., of any colour but piebald and skewbald. They are wonderful children's ponies, tending to be less shy than some other breeds from more remote areas, and their narrowness of conformation makes them especially suitable for the shorter legs of child riders.

Shetland

Smallest of all the breeds of ponies, the Shetland has been in more danger than most of being treated as a toy, or at best, a large dog. Although hardy, it needs similar care to other ponies, and is especially useful for very small children because of its size, provided the pony is properly schooled and handled first. They are extraordinarily strong for their size, and since their diet could consist merely of seaweed during a hard winter in their native islands north of Scotland, they may certainly be placed among the hardiest of ponies. They are exceptionally long-lived.

Shetlands should not exceed 42 inches, and the best are usually about 39 inches; there is no colour limitation in the breed specification, but many are black or brown. They have particularly thick winter coats, and beautifully silky coats in summer, with abundant, flowing manes, forelocks and tails. They perform well in harness but are not generally good riding ponies because of their small size and strength.

Welsh

Welsh ponies are probably just about at the top of the popularity hit parade for ponies nowadays. This is largely because of their tremendous range of usefulness, allied to their specially appealing appearance and character. Welsh ponies are divided into four sections A–D, with particular characteristics associated with each type.

A: the Welsh mountain pony, which must be no higher than 12 hh., probably derives from the Celtic pony which roamed the Welsh mountains long before recorded history in these islands. They are often grey, but most other colours are found, although piebalds and skewbalds are not eligible for registration. There is a brightness and gaiety about the Welsh pony which is especially attractive. It is difficult to resist the claims of its admirers that it is 'the world's most beautiful pony'. Their combination of hardiness and intelligence with docility makes them highly suitable for children.

Welsh Mountain Pony: one of the most successful breeds in the world, the Welsh Mountain Pony has a wonderful action. The Welsh breeds are strong, dependable and make good children's ponies.

B: Welsh ponies up to 13.2 hh. come within this section, and these are ideal riding ponies with quality and good action, plus the pony characteristics of hardiness and intelligence. They may have earlier Arab, Thoroughbred or even hackney blood, which has given them the increased scope and size, making them ideal second ponies for children once they have outgrown those of 12 hh. These Welsh ponies often make particularly good hunters for children, holding their own in grass vale country as well as moorlands.

C: Welsh ponies of cob type, between 12 and 13.2 hh., may be eligible for registration in this section, if approved. The exact origin of the Welsh cob remains shrouded in mystery, but it was well established as a breed by the fifteenth century. These smaller cobs came from Breconshire and Radnorshire; they have nice pony heads, and pony character, with well-developed knees, and are fast trotters with a fairly high knee action. While being well suited to harness work, they are excellent ride and drive animals.

D: Welsh cobs above 13.2 hh. came originally from Cardiganshire and Pembrokeshire. They combine the above-mentioned qualities with greater scope and strength, and may be as high as 15 hh., although no official height limit is set. All the best have the good constitution, hard flinty bone, courage, activity and equable temperament which has made this breed so popular in general. The Welsh cob is rightly described as an ideal family horse, being strong enough to carry a man, yet quiet enough to be a safe ride for a young girl.

2 *Making Friends*

If you are lucky, one way you may find a useful pony is by asking someone knowledgeable to recommend one locally. They should know the pony very well, its abilities, manners and performance, and how bad are its faults, since no pony is perfect.

Because young riders grow, they cannot keep ponies as long as adults may keep horses. Some families keep ponies for several years as there are younger brothers and sisters. But good ponies do come on to the market when they have been outgrown and there is an excellent chance that you will find one.

If you see a good pony at a show or a Pony Club rally you can always ask the owner to let you know when it might be sold so you can, hopefully, have a chance to purchase before it is advertised. Owners of good ponies which, sadly, they must sell are usually fairly strict about their new homes, as they want them to be well cared for.

My daughter's first ponies were all loaned to her. They were all marvellous ponies, and their devoted owners would never have sold them. Fortunately, their owners realized, when their children had grown out of them, that they would be happier if they continued to be ridden regularly, rather than being put into early retirement.

Finding Your Pony

If you mention you are looking for a pony to the

District Commissioner of your branch of the Pony Club and members' parents, this often produces the pony best suited to you. Your instructor in the Pony Club may be able to match you as a rider to a particular pony.

Advertisements in *Horse and Hound* magazine and some local papers are the way many ponies are found. Study these carefully and remember it is generally what is not written about a pony that is most important. An advertisement should state that a pony is sound, genuine and traffic proof. The advertisement should also confirm that it is good to catch, load into a horse box, and clip, and give the price and telephone number. If the price is not stated you can guess that it may be expensive.

When you telephone to ask for further information about the pony it is a good policy either then or when you see it to ask for a reference.

This means asking for the name of someone you can speak to who will recommend the pony. It could be an instructor in the Pony Club, a judge, the Secretary of your local Hunt, or any other experienced pony person. This will give you an unbiased opinion of the pony, and will prove invaluable. If the pony is genuine, people will not mind at all being asked, and will put you in contact with several people.

At an auction you are purchasing an unknown pony and you have little time and limited facilities for trying out the pony. Very good ponies are bought at auctions but it is best to leave pony buying from this source to the experienced horseman.

When you are buying a pony it is important not to be in a hurry. It is far better to miss a few weeks' riding activities than to buy, and then be unable to sell, an unsuitable pony. Safety is vital in buying a pony, and it is worth taking every precaution to check that your new pony's temperament and behaviour are not dangerous.

Viewing a Pony

When you have arranged a time to see a pony you will feel very excited. Try not to get carried away, and buy the first pony you see on impulse. All ponies are easy to buy, but only the good ones are easy to sell. You do not want to get stuck with an unsuitable pony.

Try to take a friend along with you, preferably someone more experienced who knows how you ride, where you are going to keep the pony and what you want to do with it. Your riding school instructor, Pony Club instructor, or livery yard owner may be pleased to come with you. Most horsey people always enjoy seeing ponies and horses for sale.

You may decide to go on your own first of all, but good ponies do get sold quickly. You may be very disappointed that the pony you have set your heart on has been sold before you could see it again.

When you arrive to see the pony, go into his loose-box with him. See how he behaves. First impressions are important. He should look confident and relaxed, not cheeky or nervous. Take special note of his eyes and ears. Beware ponies who look at you suspiciously, lay their ears back, or turn their hindquarters towards you. This is a sign of threatening behaviour and the pony might just do something worse. Ideally, it should come over to you nicely, interested in what is happening. If he barges into you or through the door you may be in for trouble.

The owner will put the head collar on and you can then ask to see the pony outside standing on a level piece of ground. Have a good look over him, and study his conformation and condition. He should look well covered, but not fat. If his ribs show then he is too poor and he may be a bad doer, needing special attention in feeding. This can be difficult for inexperienced owners. This condition can also suggest that a pony has a nervous disposition, burning up its energy too quickly.

Ask the owner to lead the pony at a walk, then trot straight towards you, past you and away, still in a straight line. You can study his action, and check whether he moves straight.

You will have to study many ponies to gain the experience required to assess conformation and movement, but this comes with practice. More important at first, it pays to get your eye in with regard to the type of pony you want. If you have been wanting a pony for some time you can carefully observe all the different ponies at shows, your riding school or the Pony Club. You can also look at every pony observing conformation and movement so that you gain experience.

Always ask the owners questions about the pony. Lots of things will come to mind, so do not be afraid to ask and make sure you understand the answers. Take a notebook with you if you will find it helpful.

It is just possible that you may be sold a pony that cannot carry out the purpose it was required for. If this is the case you may have to resort to legal action unless the person you bought him from will take him back. Witnesses and notes are most helpful in these cases. These incidents are rare, but they do happen. We are referring to pony mares that are found to be in foal, ponies with behavioural vices which the seller stated they were free from, and ponies on pain killing drugs to mask unsoundness.

You must ask whether the pony has any vices. These include behavioural problems like weaving, crib biting and windsucking. These bad habits are apparent when the pony is at rest. Weaving means throwing his head from side to side, usually over the stable door. Crib biting is when the pony holds on to the stable or fencing with his mouth and grunts, flexing the muscles under his throat; and windsucking is when he holds on to stabling or fencing and sucks in air.

These vices affect the pony's condition as he will

stand exhibiting this behaviour for some time instead of eating. The habits greatly lessen the pony's value. Fortunately, these vices are not as common as they have been in the past, and they do not affect ponies as much as horses, but you should be aware that they can occur and they are very serious faults.

Ask the reason for the sale, and how long the pony has been in the present ownership. There are some good reasons for sale: being outgrown, moving house, a change in personal circumstances or a teenager losing interest, but do delve to find out the true reason. You want to make sure the pony has not been recently purchased, found to be below standard and quickly being sold again.

Many good ponies are purchased from dealers. If you go to a dealer, make sure he or she has a good reputation. The disadvantage is that the dealer may not have known the pony for long, but he may be willing to take the pony back if it proves unsuitable for you. Do get this established first of all.

Ask about the pony's feed, tack, stable routine, shoeing and veterinary history.

Watching the Pony Being Ridden

The next stage is for the pony to be tacked up, and ridden by his present rider. The pony should allow his rider to tack him up without any trouble. Watching him being ridden will give you a good idea of how he goes, and how he behaves. He will be shown off to appear at his very best. Ask when he was last exercised. If he has been shown to several other purchasers he will be well used to what he is doing, and might even be getting tired. If he has not been exercised for a day or two and been turned out, he may be feeling fresh, so make allowances.

His present rider knows how to control the pony well, and understands him, so he will probably make everything look easy.

If there are any problems at this stage then the outlook will be bleak for you unless you have more experience than the rider in question. There can be enough problems with strange ponies, so do not take on too much of a challenge. Make a mental note as to whether the rider looks happy and is riding with little effort. Here are some problems of which you should be aware:

Napping

This is where the pony does not move willingly in the direction you want. This is a serious fault in some ponies. Ponies are intelligent and always seem to know where to find home and food. Watch out for a tendency to pull towards the gate leading out of the paddock where you are trying the pony. The same applies in the stable yard, or the road near the stables. If the pony naps you can be sure he will always look for an opportunity and this can occur when you are near a collecting ring or a group of ponies. Sometimes he will stop altogether and refuse to go forwards. Strong riding can improve the pony but you will always have to expect this when riding him. My first pony (14.2 hh.) napped, he was a good pony but I always had to remember to use my legs strongly when I thought I could read his mind.

If a pony pulls too much at this stage, you can be sure he will always be a puller. Nothing is more frightening for young riders than a very strong puller. Even if you put a more effective bit in his mouth, you may find the pony will pull even harder. Do not forget that ponies are bound to pull more out hunting or hacking with other ponies, so a pony that pulls hard when ridden at home is bound to be unsuitable.

Rearing is Dangerous

A pony which rears should not be kept. It is a very serious vice indeed. If a pony half plunges forward (fly bucking) then this is quite bad enough, but a full rear standing up on the hind legs is extremely dangerous. A pony that rears habitually should be put down. There is a big risk of serious injury, sometimes fatal if the pony goes right over backwards. You should ask if the pony has ever reared, and the answer should be a horrified 'no' at the very thought.

Bucking

Many ponies buck occasionally when they are feeling well. This should not be a frequent habit, because it is worrying for young riders. Once or twice with exuberance is not too alarming, but a pony that bucks at any opportunity will be a problem.

Traffic Proof?

You should also receive a very strong confirmation that the pony is good in traffic. This should apply when he is on his own, in company, on busy roads with cars, lorries, motor bikes and tractors. A pony that is not 100 per cent traffic proof is not suitable for a young rider.

Quiet to Clip, Shoe and Box?

Ask whether he is good to clip, shoe and box. Again the majority of ponies are good in all these respects but you really do not want one that is not. If you are competing and the pony is exceptional you may decide to overlook one of these problems but you will find difficulties looking after the pony.

Watching the Pony Jump

You can rest assured that the pony will be well used to the fences tried out in front of you, so his performance ought to be perfect. He should jump calmly, but willingly, tucking up his front legs neatly. He should go on at the fences, but not pull, and must be easy to stop afterwards.

It is not sufficient to watch the pony over one or two little show jumps. Ask to see him over a few natural fences as well. Note how he jumps water and ditches. A good pony should tackle these unhesitatingly. If the pony is regularly used for competition work you may see his photographs over cross-country fences.

Riding the Pony Yourself

If you are still interested in the pony at this point, you can ride him. If you do not think he will be suitable it is better to explain and leave.

You may be nervous riding a strange pony in front of others, so there is no need to do any more than you want to with him. A walk, trot, canter are quite enough, making sure that you can pull up quietly. If you feel insecure at any stage, do say so and stop.

Owners of a good pony which they value as a friend of the family will be examining you, as they will want the pony to go to a good, knowledgeable home where he will be happy. You may all feel that the partnership will not work. You may be too small or inexperienced for the pony.

It may be obvious that he would not be big enough for you for very long, and he would have to be sold again. Many fond owners do not like their loved ponies to be sold on continuously, and will obviously want a home where he can stay for some years, perhaps with a younger sister or brother growing up.

Try the pony out on the roads, in traffic. You may be able to ride out with another pony. It is doubtful whether the owners would let you ride far away from them on a strange pony. I would not, until I knew the rider was capable.

If there is another pony available, you can see how he behaves in company. Stop and let the other pony go on. He should wait quietly until you ask him to move on. The same applies when you ask him to ride on away from the other pony. This is a good test.

Agreeing the Price

If you have firmly made up your mind to buy the pony then you will have to agree on a price. At this stage you should not have any doubts about him: there should be no 'ifs' or 'buts'. You should have decided he is perfect for you.

Most sellers ask more than they would be prepared to accept as they know buyers will make them an offer on the price. However, some will stick at the asking price. You may be able to agree that the price includes some tack or rugs, or perhaps includes transport of the pony to you.

It is up to you to see what you can do in the way of negotiation. I would add here that sellers of good ponies they have had in the family for some time are understandingly reluctant to sell them. People can be easily upset about buyers haggling over the price, so try and do this as tactfully as possible.

It is not necessary to leave a deposit, but you can do this if you feel there is much demand for the pony and there would be a danger of losing him to someone else. Generally a 10 per cent deposit will be fine, and if you pay cash you should receive a receipt.

Vetting

Your offer for the pony should be subject to a veterinary examination. We recommend your pony is vetted. Only a vet can see whether the pony's heart and eyes are in order, and he will confirm your views on whether the pony is sound.

It is quite easy to miss something in the pony's soundness, so do not be alarmed if he suggests something you had not noticed. That is what you have asked him for.

A vetting is not a guarantee. A veterinary certificate states that in the vet's opinion the pony was sound for your purpose on the date he saw him.

If you already have a vet ask him to recommend another vet in the area where the pony is being sold. It may be too costly for your vet to travel there. Ask for an estimate of the cost involved. The seller's vet should not examine the pony on your behalf; obviously it is much better to employ an independent vet.

Your vet will ask for what purpose you require the pony. Generally, ponies are intended for all-round riding, but you should tell your vet if you wish to do much competing. He will assess whether the pony will stand up to the work required.

Try to be present when the vetting takes place, so that the vet can explain everything to you. It will be much clearer than by telephone.

The vet will first see the pony at rest in the stable. He will take a description and note of his markings for identification. He will examine him to see his conformation, then feel him to check all muscles, joints and tendons are healthy. He will look out for any swellings and abnormalities.

He will then check his heart and lungs with his stethoscope, and his eyes with an opthalmoscope to see they are normal. He will have a look at his teeth to age him, and examine his feet and shoeing to make sure his feet are in good order.

The vet will ask for the pony to be walked and trotted up, as you did when you first saw him. He will check that the pony is sound, and that there is nothing untoward with his action that would affect him for the riding you wish to do.

The pony is next ridden at a fast canter, and when he is blowing, the vet will listen to his breathing and heart rate to make sure these are normal at work.

The pony is then rested in the stable for about ten minutes and brought out again. This is to ensure he does not stiffen in any way when cooled down. He will be walked and trotted up again to see whether he has suddenly become lame with work. He will then be turned in tight circles, and moved backwards to make sure he can move properly and use all parts of his limbs. He will be given a spavin test at this point; his hind leg is held up sharply for a couple of minutes and then released. The pony should move away normally.

Vetting is generally a worrying time for the owners. They are concerned a vet will find something wrong with the pony that they have not noticed. It is awful to find there is something wrong with your pony that you had not realized. A vetting is also confirmation that the pony will be capable of work in the future. Again, it is worrying for the owners to think their pony may possibly have limited life ahead.

If you wish to take out an insurance policy then ask your vet to issue a veterinary certificate for insurance purposes, which your insurance company will require.

Insurance

We recommend you have your pony insured. Most insurance policies cover veterinary fees, so if your pony becomes ill, lame or you need to call the vet for advice, you will not have to worry about affording the fees. Your pony might even have to undergo X-rays or an operation or stay in a veterinary hospital. Worse, he might die or become unable to be ridden. This is too sad to think about, but it can happen.

Your insurance should also cover third party negligence. If an accident is caused through the pony's fault then you would be liable to pay damages which could be serious and expensive. The pony may indirectly cause an accident through escaping from his field and going across a road. He may be unhurt but cars may crash avoiding him.

If you decide against insuring your pony, do ensure that he is at least covered for third party insurance. You can take out a smaller policy, or can sometimes include this on your parents' household policy. If you belong to the British Horse Society then you will automatically have this insurance included in your membership.

Loss of Use Clause

You can insure for loss of use of your pony. He may become unable to be ridden or to compete as you intended. This mainly applies to competition ponies; eventing, show jumping or show ponies.

Do not insure the pony for more than you paid for him, which is likely to be the market value. Insurance companies will only pay out the market value in the event of a claim. Your saddlery and your trailer can be included in the insurance, and this is a good idea as they are items which could be stolen.

3 *Life Style*

There are several choices open to you in keeping your pony. The choice you make will depend on your budget, and on the time available for looking after him.

Looking after a pony is always time consuming but if your pony is stabled the daily work is especially demanding. If you are at school and have homework, you will not have sufficient time for this, unless you have a parent willing to help, or can afford to employ a full-time groom.

It is much easier to keep your pony out in a field all the year round. This is sometimes called 'at grass' or 'living out'. Another alternative is to combine both methods, keeping the pony out for part of the year and stabled at other times, or keeping the pony indoors at night and out during the day in winter; perhaps vice versa in summer.

Ponies are happy living out at grass all the year, but if you wish to compete regularly during the summer holidays you should plan to keep him in a stable at nights. This will make him fitter, as he will not be eating grass all the time.

A converted shelter or barn can be used temporarily as a stable. Ponies are generally more controllable rides if they are turned out for a few hours during the day.

If you are competing and hunting regularly, it is best to have your pony stabled during the Christmas, Easter and summer holidays, and out at grass during the term-time. Otherwise, a stable is useful for the night before shows or hunting.

One major danger in keeping ponies out at grass is laminitis, the disease known as 'fever of the feet'. It is caused by an excessive diet of rich grass and lack of exercise.

You will probably have seen the moorlands where our native pony breeds originate. You will notice how sparse and poor the grass is. The ponies have to walk at least a few miles each day to obtain their forage. Unfortunately, there is often a worming problem in the moorland areas which causes many of the ponies to be thin, but generally the moorland has been sufficient to maintain native ponies for hundreds of years.

This background is important to understand. As we have already described, the riding pony of today is derived from the native breeds who were developed on very sparse, natural grazing.

Therefore, when your pony has access to very lush growing grass without having to move very far, he is likely to get laminitis which makes him almost rooted to the spot, unable to move, with hot feet. His blood system cannot cope with the rich diet.

It is vital to restrict the grazing diet of your pony from April to July when the grass is growing in abundance. You will either need a very small paddock or stable where he can be kept when the grass is at its most lush.

Do not think that because the grass in your pony's field does not look very plentiful, he will be all right; he has obviously eaten it all. You must be cruel to be kind, and restrict his intake. Most ponies are too fat in the early summer months. We discuss laminitis further in the diseases and ailments chapter (Chapter 8).

In the wild state a pony can shelter under, or by, large trees and hedges, boulders and rocks, and can use the sheltered sides of hills for protection against the weather. Large trees and thick hedges are ideal, but sadly our countryside is devoid of these in some areas. If the field in which you intend to keep your pony does not have proper shade and shelter, then you will need to provide a shed or stable.

At Grass

Your pony's field offers as natural an environment as possible, similar to that experienced by wild ponies.

The field should be about five acres in size for three or four ponies. If your pony is turned out all the year, you should have the use of two fields, so that one can be rested. Small pony paddocks or fenced off areas of the garden are not suitable for all the year use. There are no strict guide lines as to the size of the field. It all depends on the quality of the grass, and the size, type and condition of the ponies to be turned out.

As we have indicated, most ponies are 'good doers', but if your pony is a breedy, rangy type it will need more food to keep it in good condition.

The grass should be short and thick; field maintenance is necessary to keep the grass like this. If you own the field you will have to arrange for it to be topped; the coarse, long patches cut off. These areas are not nutritional, and appear where the ponies foul. If the field is small, and there are many droppings, you should collect them up with a wheelbarrow and dispose of them outside the field. They increase the spread of worms and stop the grass growing; the field becomes infested with worms and is 'horse sick'.

Sheep are valuable to keep the grass growing well and to sweeten the grazing. They eat all the areas of grass ponies do not like, promoting better grass growing and their little cloven feet constantly harrow the grass.

It is not ideal to keep beef bullocks with ponies; the bullocks constantly break through fences and it is difficult for children to handle their ponies with these large cattle around, as they are often unruly.

If you rent the field, the farmer should carry out the maintenance of the field, so confirm this when you agree the price of the rent.

The field will need spraying to kill dangerous weeds, but some sprays are poisonous until there has been a rainfall, so check before turning ponies out. You should have a knowledge of poisonous plants: ragwort is particularly poisonous for ponies and horses; it is a tall yellow flowering plant. Yew, the evergreen tree, and acorns are also poisonous; you should collect acorns when they fall in the autumn. Ponies do not generally eat anything they consider suspicious, but you can never be sure. Never let them graze where they can eat yew leaves.

Fencing

Effective fencing is vital, especially if the field is near a road. Ideally there should be a small holding area, or yard, between the field and the road so your pony will not escape into the traffic. It is sometimes difficult to groom and tack up ponies in their own field, but they seem to understand they must stand quietly when led through the gate to a small enclosed area.

You can use this area in which to mount your pony instead of doing so in the road, or in the field where ponies are sometimes naughty.

Bear this in mind for schooling and jumping as well. Ponies become familiar with their own field and sometimes take advantage of young riders there.

Good fencing is expensive. Post and rails, or hedges, are best, but for economic reasons plain wire stapled to posts is satisfactory. The lowest strand should not allow the pony to get his foot over and the wire must be taut, not slack, or he will get caught up.

Barbed wire is dangerous for ponies, but it is used a great deal in the countryside. Your pony may be fortunate and escape injury, but there are often bad accidents with barbed wire. Ponies tend to get hung up in it, and the resulting flesh wounds are usually serious, requiring stitching or veterinary supervision.

If you do use it, make sure it is not slack as it is then more likely to cause harm. Ponies push their legs over the lower strands and get caught up. Check your ponies even more carefully if their field is fenced with barbed wire.

Erecting a fence is a job for an expert, but to give you some idea of what it involves, you should allow for six-foot posts driven into the ground for two feet and at a distance from every eight or ten feet. It is vital the posts are erected properly as they are subject to strain from the weight and force of ponies. Once one post falls over they all do. If your father intends to put up the fencing you should impress upon him how effective it has to be.

Electric fences can be used to divide a field to rest each part in turn. This type of fencing is not suitable as a perimeter fence. Once a pony has had an electric shock he is usually frightened of wire forever; even small lengths of it, lying on the ground out riding.

The field gate should be properly supported, and easy to open and shut. It can be difficult enough to catch your pony and lead it through the gate with other ponies around, and it is even worse if you have to struggle with the gate as well.

Ideally the gate should be padlocked to prevent your pony being stolen, or hooligans letting him out.

It is common sense that you should pick up anything in the field which could harm your pony. This might include old pieces of corrugated iron, cans and oil drums and polythene sheeting.

Water

Ponies living out drink gallons of water daily, and it is very cruel to keep them short. Buckets of water in the field are not adequate. The best solution is a piped water supply, with a trough which fills automatically. Otherwise you may have to fill a trough with a hosepipe. Old baths can be used, but sharp edges should be padded. Water troughs become stagnant, so you must clean them out with a stiff brush. Do not use detergent; it is not necessary and it is difficult to rinse.

The field may have a stream, but streams can dry up. Similarly, hoses can leak and ballcocks in automatic troughs can stop working, so keep checking the water supply.

Happy in Company
Most ponies are happiest when they have company. Some ponies are content when turned out alone, but many never settle. It is wise to keep ponies together if they get on well together; if you frequently turn out strange ponies among them they will have to keep getting to know one another. Be prepared for a kicking match when you turn a new pony out for the first time with others. It is best to remove the hind shoes, and try to avoid turning a mare out with several geldings: mares can cause trouble.

Donkeys can make good companions for ponies but check regularly whether the donkey has lungworm. Your vet should do this before the donkey is turned out. Donkeys are prone to lungworm and this can be transferred to your pony, resulting in a bad cough.

Checking Your Pony at Grass
You must get into the habit of visiting your pony, and checking him, every day. If you are at school, and it is too dark in the winter, you will have to arrange this with a parent or friend. It is not enough just to look at him from a distance over the fence. You must go up to him, look him all over for cuts

and swellings, check that he is grazing, and appears to be in a healthy condition.

If he is lying down when you call you must encourage him to get up; if he shows that this is difficult, it may mean he is hurt, or has colic. You must regularly observe your pony closely to ensure he is happy and well.

Stabling Your Pony

There are many reasons why you may wish to stable your pony. You may decide to have him close to hand for convenience. Perhaps you will wish to compete regularly, and work your pony hard. This means he would be best given concentrated feeds, avoiding being full of grass all the time. It is difficult to get a pony very fit while out at grass.

Other reasons for stabling your pony could be that he is ill or lame and requires box-rest, or he may not thrive being out all the winter.

It is more expensive to have a pony stabled and much more hard work. Your pony will require daily exercise, either by being ridden, lunged or turned out for a few hours.

Once you have decided to keep him in during the winter it is unfair suddenly to turn him out without proper acclimatization. You will have to organize extra help to look after him when you are away or ill.

Livery Yards

There are alternatives to having your own stable. One solution is to use a good livery yard where horses and ponies can be kept for a weekly fee. This can be expensive as your pony will be looked after entirely by the livery yard. If you can afford it you may decide it is best, but you will never really learn how to look after your pony.

Part-livery arrangements work out well, as you can carry out some of the care, and the livery yard will look after your pony the rest of the time. This is sensible for the first-time owner. The livery yard will be able to advise you on areas of pony care that you have not encountered before, particularly if there is an emergency. Make sure the livery yard is of good repute; some are much better than others.

There are some yards where you rent the stable and possibly the grazing, and look after the pony totally yourself. This arrangement is generally good, but bear in mind that you will have to visit your pony three times a day.

There is another sort of livery known as a working livery, where a riding stables will look after your pony in return for using it for lessons and rides. The drawback is that the stables will wish to use him at the weekends and holidays when you will require him. We know of a friend who had a good arrangement with a stables at a boarding school whereby the pony was used during the term time by the school, and during the holidays by the owner.

Stables

If you have a stable, also known as a loose box, or you can rent one, you are fortunate. If not, and you decide to build one, you will first have to apply to your local council for planning permission. Detailed plans have to be submitted, and remember in addition to the stable, you need hay storage in a covered barn or lean-to, tack room, feed shed and muck heap area.

There are some good pre-fabricated stables on the market which are advertised widely. If you decide on this sort, then your parents must help you to shop around and work out which type is best for you. Alternatively, a local builder can erect a stable from your own plans.

The siting is important. The drainage will be helped considerably if the stable is on higher ground. Otherwise you and your pony will be immersed in mud and water in the winter.

Do not just build a small stable for a small pony.

You will grow and may need a horse later, so make sure it will be big enough. Ideally, it should be at least twelve by ten feet (3.6m × 3m) with a height of at least eight feet (2.4m).

Ponies do not often get cast (stuck on their side after rolling) but small stables do encourage this. If your pony does get cast, you must rope his legs and pull him back over. Do not attempt to do this on your own, and stand well clear.

Stalls are not suitable for ponies. They are old-fashioned, and require a different method of stable management. They are used by the Army and the Police where there are different routines, but nowadays they are seldom used for hunters, or riding horses. Garden sheds are certainly not strong enough for stabling.

Loose boxes can be built of timber, concrete blocks or brick. Whatever you choose it should be substantial. A lean-to may be built on to the side of the stable for hay and straw storage, and this can be cheaper if corrugated iron is used. Whatever you use do not forget that lorries bringing hay and straw tend to be large and to deliver a load it will be necessary to drive the lorry up to the barn. The same applies to the muck heap. When you arrange for collection from a farmer or mushroom grower, they will need access right up to the muck heap.

The flooring can be concrete or chalk, and should not be slippery. Chalk which needs renewing, is generally used in studs for brood mares and foals so they do not hurt themselves on the concrete. The door should be strong to prevent the pony knocking it down. Stable doors take a lot of battering. There should be bolts at the top and bottom on the outside so that your pony cannot undo both of them and escape.

You need two sturdy ring attachments; one for tying up the pony, and one for the haynet. Hay racks, mangers and water bowls are convenient if they happen to be installed, but for ponies you can easily improvise with a water bucket, preferably one not easy to knock over, and a feed bin which can also be used in a paddock.

Rainwater should flow into a gutter, and then into a soakaway drain. A concrete strip in front of the stable is an advantage, as the area in front of the stable will become muddy in winter.

You will have to provide piped water within easy reach of the stable; it is not practical to carry water from elsewhere.

Electricity is a boon, for light and for electric clippers. In the winter months stable routine can be quite difficult in the dark. Torches do not give enough light. Ponies should not be able to reach either the light bulbs or the switches.

Any windows should be covered inside with wire netting, and make sure there is nothing to damage your pony. Sometimes old nails or jagged edges are left on walls. A pony is very curious, and he will have time in the stable to explore everything.

Mucking Out

At night your pony will require a thick bed of straw to lie on, but during the day he only needs a thin layer of straw to stop him slipping on the floor of the stable. The stable will need mucking out each day.

If your pony has an allergy to straw and reacts badly by coughing, you may be advised by your vet to use wood shavings or shredded paper instead. These can be bought from a timber merchant; you need to provide thick bedding as it tends to compress with the pony's weight. The stable will still need mucking out each day.

For mucking out you will need:
A long handled, long pronged stable fork or pitchfork.
A large stiff stable broom.
A shovel.

A wheelbarrow or large muck sack.

A rake if you need to collect up the straw blown around the stable yard or garden.

When you muck out you remove all the droppings and wet straw bedding. Remove all the droppings with the shovel. Clear out a corner of the stable and sweep it clean. With the fork, sift through the bedding and put all the clean straw in the corner. All the wet bedding goes in the wheelbarrow with the droppings. When you have finished, sweep the floor.

You can change corners each day so each part of the stable gets a thorough clean. It is not advisable to leave the straw round the edges unsorted. Many people do so for quickness. It encourages rats and mice, and it is much more difficult to clean when you get round to doing it.

If you are mucking out with your pony in the stable, tie him up on a short length and make him move over when you want him to. Talk to him and tell him to 'Get over'. Make him stand still, not tread all over you. Ponies can suddenly rush out over the wheelbarrow if they are not tied up properly.

Take the wheelbarrow to the muck heap which should be kept as neat and square as possible. You may find a gardening nursery or a farmer willing to come to collect it every few months.

If you are mucking out shavings you should remove all the damp bedding. A bedding of wet shavings heats up considerably, and it is bad for your pony's feet. You will have to arrange for the shavings to be collected or the muck heap can be burnt.

Ideally you should leave the stable to dry before putting in more bedding. You may find it best to put in extra straw when you feed your pony for the night. The new straw should be sifted through and well banked up around the sides and the corners, so that your pony does not rub or knock his limbs against the wall, especially when he is lying down. Finally, sweep back the bed to about two feet inside the door. Ponies do not need straw right up to the door, and it will only trail across the yard every time your pony comes out of his stable.

When you muck out the stable, clean out the water bucket and fill the pony's haynet.

4 *What's on the Menu?*

The natural food for a pony is grass. When stabled, or when grass becomes scarce, you feed your pony dried grass which is hay.

Grass is plentiful in the spring and autumn. Sometimes you will need to feed your pony hay in August after a hot summer with a drought when the grass has turned brown. You will certainly have to feed hay in the winter months, especially when the ground is frozen, or there is snow.

To give your pony extra energy when the weather is cold, and to keep him warm, short concentrated feeds can be added to his diet in the form of oats, bran and barley.

The main point to remember when feeding ponies is that most thrive well, and it is all too easy to overfeed them. Not only is this wasteful, but it causes ill health, especially laminitis, and it makes some ponies very difficult to ride; they get 'above themselves' and behave badly.

Ponies have small stomachs and need to eat concentrated feeds little and often. It is better to feed two small feeds per day than one large one.

Grass

There are many varieties of grass. The best is the short, close cropped variety of permanent pasture. If you compare the grazing in most fields with the sparse moorland that the native ponies have lived on for generations, then you will understand how plentiful is the grass in your pony's field. You should never give your pony grass cuttings, as these can ferment and cause colic.

Hay

Good hay should be sweet smelling. Dusty hay or yellow hay should not be fed, especially if your pony is prone to coughing. For such ponies, hay should always be dampened by putting it in a trough of water before feeding.

Seed hay is cut from specially grown mixtures of grasses. It is nutritious for ponies and generally not too rich. Meadow hay is cut from permanent pasture, and has a sweet smell. This is the most suitable hay for ponies in average work. If you are only riding your pony at weekends because of the dark nights in the winter, then meadow hay is sufficient. Clover hay tends to be too rich for ponies, and is generally given to racehorses.

New hay that has just been made can give a pony colic. Hay should be fed when it has been cut at least six months; it will last up to eighteen months.

Hay is usually sold by the half ton, the ton, or by the bale. There are about forty bales to the ton. You can buy hay from a farmer or your corn merchant. Avoid hay that appears mouldy as it was probably stacked before it was dry. If you buy your hay from your livery yard then they will be able to advise you. When storing hay, it is a good idea to stack it on pallets, keeping it off the ground to prevent the bottom bales from spoiling.

Horsehage is a cross between hay and silage; the dust is extracted before it is bagged for sale. It can be given to ponies with an allergy to hay and straw. Some ponies develop an allergy from the dust in forage which affects their breathing. If you remove the cause, their condition will usually improve.

YOUR PONY

Straw
This is the stalks of wheat, barley or oats which remain after harvesting. Straw is used for bedding, and can be stored next to your hay.

Oats
It is not necessary to give your pony oats unless he is in hard work. It is mainly used for horses. Oats make ponies feel extremely well, and hot up, making some ponies unmanageable when ridden. If you decide to feed oats, they should be crushed and not fed whole when they are less digestible.

Bran
This should be included in the main feed for stabled ponies. It acts as a laxative. It is not necessary to feed grass-kept ponies bran. Preferably you should damp the feed and allow time for it to swell. Once you

Feed for your pony: clockwise from bottom left: pony nuts, oats, bran, coarse feed, apples, chaff.

open a bag of bran use it up. Bran does not keep, and tends to go musty and mouldy.

Bran mashes are a good feed for tired or sick ponies. To make a mash, pour hot water over 2 lb of bran making it moist but not sloppy. Stir well and cover with a thick towel and leave until cool enough for your pony to eat.

Bran is also used as a poultice for ponies' feet. Your vet will advise if this is required. Hot bran is put into some sacking and tied around the leg. The action of the bran is to draw out any infection in the foot.

Pony Nuts

These provide a balanced diet for ponies, and are easy to feed as they do not need mixing or dampening. Ponies also tend to eat them all up, so there is no wastage. Nuts are quite an expensive way to feed, but they do save time and the makers provide guidance on which type is most suitable for your pony.

Coarse Feeds

A fairly new idea is the ready-to-serve horse and pony mixed feed. This is our favourite way to feed ponies, as it gives them a balanced appetizing feed. The mix contains many ingredients, including oats, nuts and molasses. Again, it is quite expensive, but can be given to stabled or grass-fed ponies. There are several different brands and strengths of this feed. Ask your corn merchant's advice so that you do not buy one that is too strong for your pony.

Barley

This should be generally boiled before consumption to aid digestion. You do not need to worry about feeding barley to your pony unless he is thin and requires fattening. It can be difficult to cook as it needs a large container, and gentle simmering for hours. It is not ideal to cook in your kitchen and requires a stable cooker.

Linseed

This MUST be soaked and boiled to form a thick jelly for feeding. It is not necessary to feed this food to your pony unless you intend to compete or show at a high level. It improves the blood and puts a bloom on the coat.

Salt Licks

Salt is a vital part of your pony's diet. You can buy a salt lick at your saddlers, or corn merchants, and keep it in the field or stable all the time. These salt licks also contain other minerals and vitamins.

Apples and Carrots

Ponies love apples and carrots in their feeds. You can often find a bag of apples or carrots which are past their best. If you ask at the green grocers they often have a supply at the back which are ideal for ponies. They make feeds more tempting if chopped up and added sometimes.

Slice apples and carrots lengthwise so they cannot get stuck in your pony's windpipe and mix them into the feed.

Ponies do not need extra minerals or vitamins added to their feed unless your vet advises.

Sudden changes in the feeding routine should be avoided. Ponies like routine, and should be fed at approximately the same time each day.

Storing Feed

The feed should be stored in feed bins or dustbins. Rats and mice are easily attracted to feed bags wherever you store them. It can be difficult to get rid of rodents, and it is unhealthy for you, as well as your pony, to have rats in the feed sheds.

WHAT'S ON THE MENU?

When to Feed and How Much

If your pony is at grass, it is best to give him his feed after exercise before you turn him out.

You will need a feed scoop to measure the amounts. Work out on the scales how many pounds are equal to your scoop. It is not sufficient to estimate by a number of scoops. All scoops vary, and

FEEDING FOR PONIES FOR PONY CLUB, SHOWS, HACKING, HUNTING, ETC:

	SUMMER AT GRASS	WINTER STABLED AT NIGHT GRASS BY DAY
12.2 hh. to 13.2 hh. pony		
Horse coarse mix	2lb	3lb
Bran	Not necessary	½–¾lb
Hay	None except if very dry and grass scarce	6lb 2 small haynets
13.2 hh. to 14.22 hh. pony		
Pony nuts or horse coarse mix	4lb	5lb
Bran	Not necessary	1lb
Hay	None except if very dry and grass scarce	8lb 2 small/medium haynets

you need to know accurately how much your pony is being fed. You may need to tell your vet one day, and it is not enough to just say two scoops of pony nuts. He will want to know how many pounds it is.

During the week in the summer term time you may find it is not necessary to feed your pony out at grass if you are not riding every day. It can be difficult to find time for riding and homework.

If your pony is stabled, then you should give him two haynets each day. The first one is best given after exercise in the morning. If you are not riding until the afternoon, then he should have a haynet in the morning, but remove it about an hour before exercise. You should not exercise your pony after feeding. It is not fair on him, and he will feel the same as you would if you played sport after a big meal.

The second haynet should be given late in the afternoon with the evening feed. Ponies generally eat all their hay up. Horses can be difficult feeders, and sometimes need encouragement to eat hay by putting it on the floor. With ponies this is not necessary, and you can save much wastage by using a haynet. When tying up a haynet, thread the end through the ring on the wall quite high up, pull it tight and then thread the end through the bottom of the haynet to secure it. Bring this up as tight as you can, and finish with a quick release knot (see p.69).

You must ensure that the empty haynet will not trail on the floor. Your pony could easily get caught up in it.

Clean, fresh water should be available all the time whether your pony is at grass or stabled. Ponies will not drink from stagnant supplies, and would rather go thirsty. Make sure you clean out the water containers regularly.

The only time to restrict your pony's water is after strenuous exercise. Just give your pony a few mouthfuls, and then wait until he has cooled down before you allow him a longer drink. He should not be subjected to fast work for half an hour after a long drink.

Every day in winter, you will have to break frozen ice on the waterbutt in the field. Broken ice will not harm your pony, and there is no need to heat the water.

5 Keeping Up Appearances

You must understand your pony in order to handle him properly. Each pony has a unique temperament and has been used to different handling in his previous ownerships.

Leading and Tying Up

We strongly suggest that you have a plain rope on the head collar which you can thread through the eye of the halter rope. There have been bad accidents with the metal clips which are so often used on the end of halter ropes sold today. These clips are sharp and can easily cut your hands and fingers, and even your face, if your pony panics and pulls back suddenly. Ponies have been known to try to chew the clips, which can result in their mouths or lips being badly cut.

Always put the head collar on by undoing the strap, putting the lower part around the pony's nose and then doing the strap up on the near side (left side).

You lead your pony from the near side. Hold the rope about ten inches from the pony's head in your right hand and the free end in your left hand. Walk alongside your pony's neck; try not to get in front, pulling him along, or you may suddenly get the back of your heels trodden on. Keep control of his head. It is easy to turn to the left by pulling his head towards you. Push his head away from you if you

KEEPING UP APPEARANCES

want to turn right. Try not to allow him suddenly to put down his head to eat.

Tie up your pony to a sensible place. Use a quick release knot (see diagram), but if you find that your pony knows how to untie this by just pulling the end, then put the end through the loop. It is best to make a small loop of binder string (from hay bales) on a fixed tying-up ring attached to a wall, in case the pony pulls back. Tie your halter rope to the string loop: if your pony panics and pulls back only the string breaks; your pony will not get hurt and nothing will break. A tug of war by a pony against an unbreakable rope attached to a fixed position can

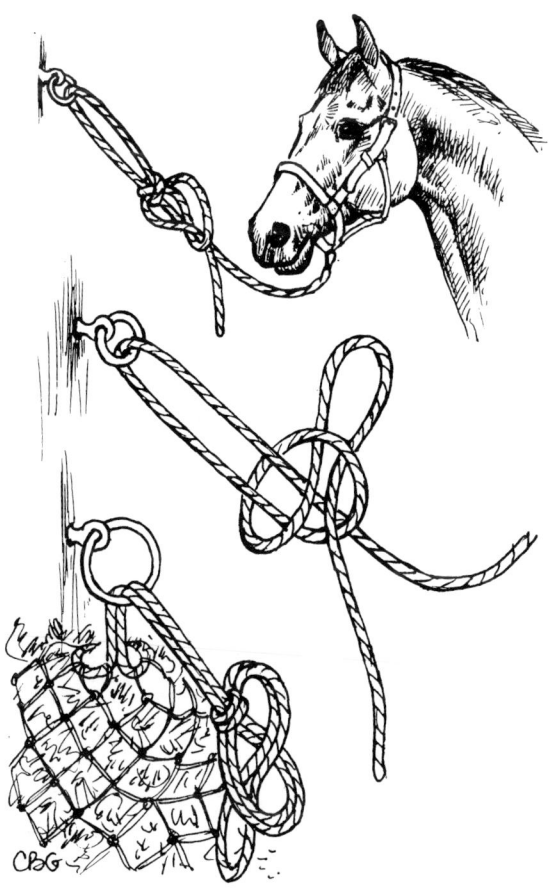

lead to panic; the pony may even fall down and hurt himself.

Choose your place to tie up with care, and try to get your pony used to one tying-up place in the stable yard, so he will understand he has to stand quietly there. Avoid places near vehicles, drains, stable equipment and the feed room. It is especially important to use breakable string if you tie him to the side of a horsebox or trailer at a show.

If your pony does panic, the use of the quick release knot on the halter rope is vital. He has obviously been frightened in the past and you will have to tie him up to a breakable string and be very patient for some time until he gets more confidence.

You should be especially careful to watch a new pony to see that he is safe while tied up. Until you know your pony is good when tied up, never leave him unattended while tethered.

In the Stable

When you go into his stable talk in a friendly manner to your pony. Do not creep up on him and startle him. Well-mannered ponies will move round to face you as you enter. Do not barge into a loose box while a strange horse or pony has his hind quarters towards you. Make him walk round to face you. You may have to do this many times before it becomes a habit. Always close the stable door behind you and latch it so that your pony does not escape. This may seem obvious but it is surprising how often people do not do this.

If your pony is difficult to catch in the stable, leave his head collar on properly adjusted. If he should turn his quarters on you in the stable and threatens to kick, he may need careful and experienced handling. Some ponies are dangerous in this respect, but if your pony is just nervous, encourage him with a titbit and make a fuss of him when you catch him. We are not generally in favour of titbits, as they can lead to bad habits; it is a nuisance when a pony is always pushing at you for food. But in some cases titbits are useful in sweetening a pony which is nervous and inclined to be on the defence in a stable.

Grooming

Grooming is for removing dirt from the coat and keeping the coat healthy and glossy.

Thorough grooming is best carried out after exercise when the pony is slightly warm, but not sweating. The cleaning and conditioning is more effective then. If you are going to a show or rally you can give your pony a good grooming the day before. You should always lightly brush your pony over before going out on exercise to remove stains so that he looks neat for riding.

Ponies at grass are often impossible to keep clean in the winter. You should only brush off dry mud, but never wash your pony in winter as his coat is then so thick that it can take more than a day to dry properly. You will also risk removing all the natural oils in his coat which help to keep him warm.

Grass-kept ponies are best put into a stable overnight before hunting, hunter trialing or Pony Club rallies. Put down a thick bed of straw which helps to dry the coat, and loosen the mud if the pony lies down. Do not shut the top door. Your pony will not feel cold, as he is used to being out, and the air circulating will help dry him. You should not put a rug on him, as it will only get filthy and stop him from drying.

You can tackle the dried mud next morning. Use a dandy brush or rubber curry comb. If you start to cough or sneeze wear a scarf over your nose and mouth to stop you inhaling the dust. If you do not have a stable then you will have to ride a wet or muddy pony. This is not such a terrible thing. Do not let it put you off riding in company; everyone else's ponies will soon be muddy in the winter conditions.

Ponies kept out at grass, and unclipped, should not be plaited. The mane will often be wet and muddy. It is a good idea to pull your pony's mane well in the autumn so there is not so much of it. It can be very messy round the reins in the winter months.

Grooming Kit

Body brush: a softer and shorter-bristled brush used to remove deeper dirt and dust. The body brush should be used for manes and tails as it will not pull the hair out.

Curry comb: the metal curry comb is used as a scraper to clean the body brush.

Dandy brush: a coarse-bristled brush, sometimes made of coloured nylon, used to clean off the dirt. It is mainly used for winter coats.

Hoof oil and brush: for oiling and conditioning the feet.

Hoof pick: a metal hook for cleaning out the feet.

Mane and tail comb: short metal combs used for pulling the mane and tail.

Rubber curry comb: used to remove the mud from a pony kept at grass.

Sponges: for cleaning the eyes, nose and dock.

Stable rubber or cloth: for final polishing (a tea towel will be less expensive).

Sweat scraper: a metal band sometimes on a wooden handle, used to remove sweat and water from the coat.

Tail bandage: a stretchy crepe bandage with ties at one end.

Water brush: a smaller, long-bristled brush used to damp down the mane and tail, clean the feet and remove mud or stable stains from the coat.

A wisp: as a rule, this is not used nowadays for general riding horses. It is made from woven hay, and used to massage the muscles and shine the coat.

KEEPING UP APPEARANCES

There are now leather-covered felt massage pads available which give the same effect, but these are not necessary for ponies unless showing or competing at a high level.

Your grooming kit is best kept in a plastic bucket or carrier with a handle which are sold in garages or DIY stores. They are easily kept clean, and we find them easier to work with than the special grooming-kit bags where you cannot see everything easily, and all the small objects tend to get buried at the bottom.

Your brushes should be washed regularly with washing powder, rinsed and left to dry, bristles downwards so that the water does not run into the wood, letting it rot. You can turn them over to dry the bristles at the end thoroughly. You cannot clean your pony properly with dirty brushes. It is a waste of time.

How to Groom

Tie up your pony in the stable. If the weather is good you can groom him outside his stable; there is more room and generally better light. If he is rugged up, leave one blanket folded over the area you are not grooming so that he does not get cold.

Start by picking out the feet with the hoof pick.

Basic grooming kit: left to right, front row: metal curry comb, body brush, rubber curry comb, hoof pick, mane comb with plaiting kit; centre row: *water brush, tail bandage;* back row: *dandy brushes, hoof oil brushes, sweat scraper, with plastic grooming-kit holder. All shown on a stable rubber.*

Pick up each foot in turn by sliding your hand down the back of each leg. If your pony does not pick his foot up straight away, tap the fetlock a couple of times with your hand as a reminder to your pony to pick his foot up and then gently hold the foot and press your weight against his shoulder.

This takes his weight off the foot and you will find he will pick his foot up. As soon as he lifts his foot, support it with your hand and hold it up.

Use the point of the hoof pick to work downwards from the heel to the toe. You must leave the central triangle of the soft parts of the frog.

Inspect the nails, and make sure the shoe is secure and that none of the nail clenches on the outer wall have risen.

Next, use the dandy brush to remove all the caked dirt, sweat marks and rain marks from your pony's coat. You can use the dandy brush in either hand and use a backwards-and-forwards way of brushing to clean all the marks off. Be careful when using the dandy brush not to attack sensitive areas of the body; it is a stiff, harsh brush and some ponies do not like it under their bellies or between their hind legs. Hold the tail when you brush the hind legs; it helps to balance you as you bend down, and will discourage your pony from kicking you. There is no such animal as a completely safe pony or horse. Even the mildest mannered animal may one day give you a nasty surprise with a kick or a bite.

It is not safe to kneel down beside your pony as you groom him. Always bend down, and be careful if you crouch down. Be ready to get out of the way quickly if your pony moves or is startled. If you stand fairly close to him, you will find he will be less likely to move around. If he does begin to fidget, talk to him and tell him to 'Get over' or 'Stand up' in a stern voice. Ponies do hear what you say, and can understand quite a lot! The tone of your voice is

KEEPING UP APPEARANCES

more important than the actual words.

Use the body brush to remove the deeper dust and dirt. Start with the mane, and make sure it is hanging on the off-side (right) of the neck. Brush it through to remove all tangles, and if it will not stay down well, damp it with the water brush.

To groom the body, start at the top of the neck with the body brush in your left hand and the metal curry comb in your right hand. Bend your left arm slightly, and when you brush, use sweeping strokes and put your weight behind each stroke, so that you brush for the best effect. Brush in the direction of the hairs of the coat. After six strokes, clean the body brush by brushing it across the teeth of the curry comb. You will be surprised how much dirt appears. You then remove this dirt when it is beginning to collect by tapping the curry comb on the ground or on the side of the stable.

For some areas of the body you may find it easier to transfer the body brush to your other hand. You

Grooming your pony with a body brush: face the tail and use the hand nearest the pony's body to hold the brush. Use short, sweeping strokes.

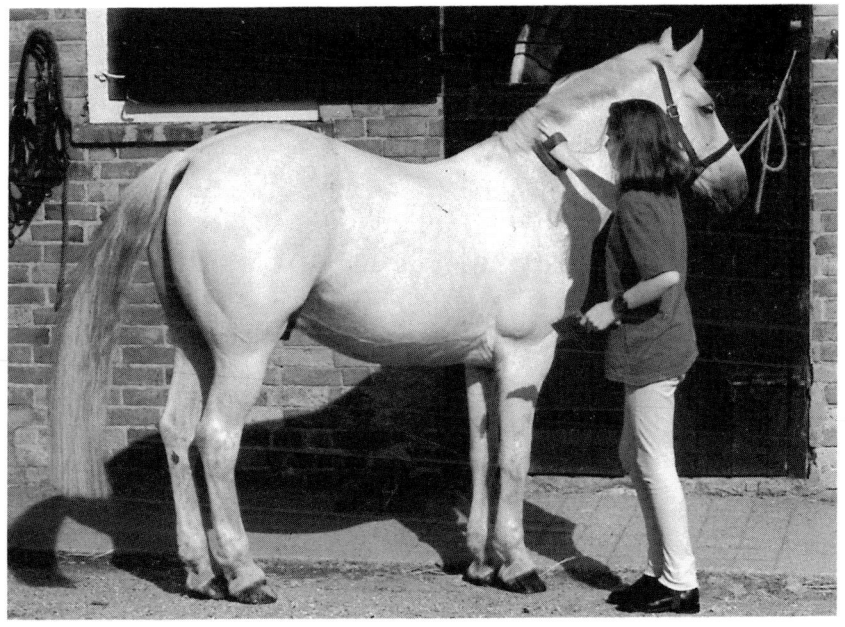

YOUR PONY

To clean the body brush scrape it across the curry comb held in your other hand.

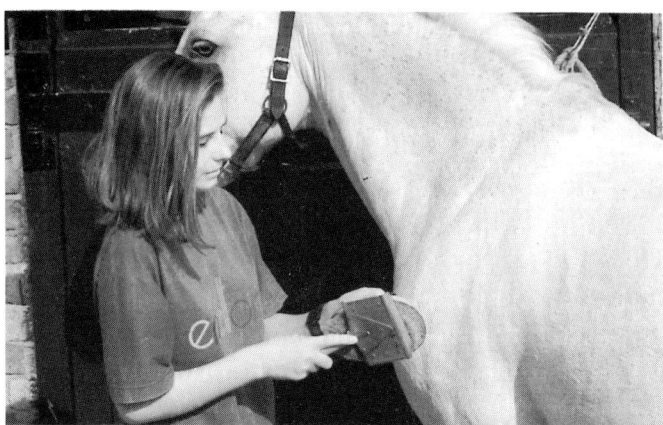

To brush your pony's head remove the headcollar noseband and use the body brush gently.

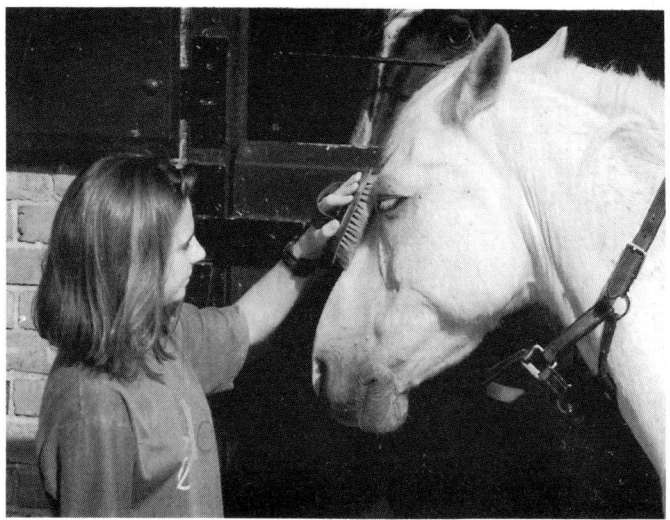

will find that grooming is a knack which gets easier the more you practise it.

Next, start on the off-side of the pony, and transfer the body brush to your right hand. If you are left-handed you may find this difficult, and it may be easier for you to keep the brush in your left hand.

Now groom the head by untying the head collar and brushing up around the neck. You do not need to hold the curry comb, so use your free hand to steady the head. Be careful you do not knock your pony's head about with the brush. Some ponies are wary of having their faces brushed, and they have usually been hit clumsily.

Finish the coat by polishing with the stable rubber, rolled into a bundle and used very slightly damp. Dampen the sponge and use to wash the corners of the eyes, muzzle and nostrils.

You should brush the tail a few strands at a time. Hold the tail with one hand and let a few strands hang down. Untangle these by brushing with the body brush, then let a few more strands hang down and brush, until the whole tail has been brushed.

Damp the top of the tail with the water brush, and then put on a tail bandage.

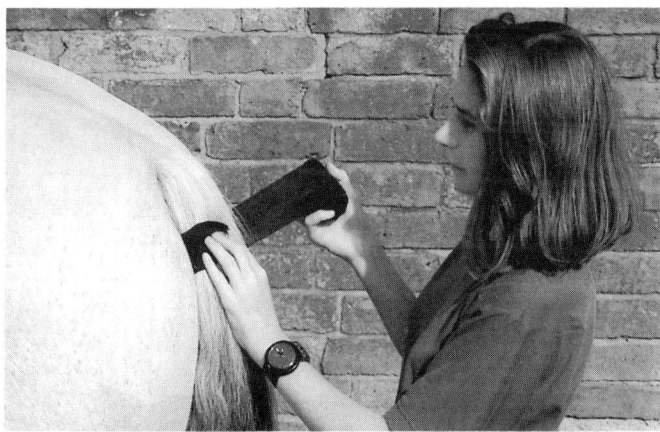

Putting on a tail bandage: lift the tail well up and stand to the side of the back legs. Start bandaging near the top.

Lift the tail up and wind the bandage firmly round so that it is secure.

Bandage right up to the top, then down towards the end of the dock (tail bone).

Secure the bandage tapes with a neat bow and tuck in the ends. This pony is also being rugged up. Double up the rug before you throw it over the withers and then pull back the top layer. It is easier to do it this way.

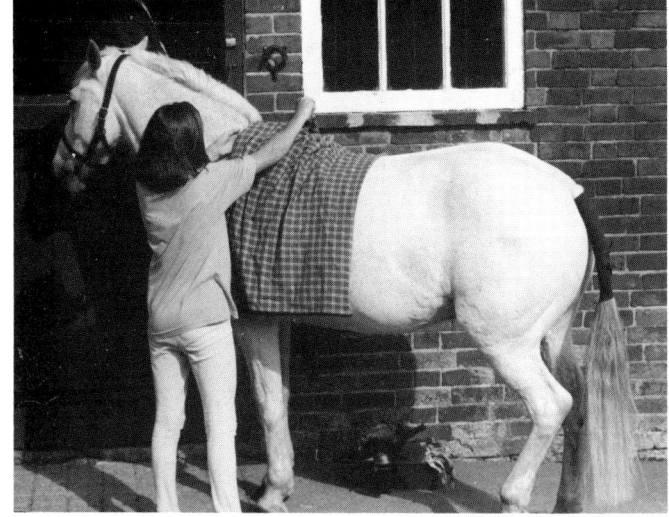

Oiling your pony's feet is the finishing touch in the process of grooming. It looks smart and benefits the feet.

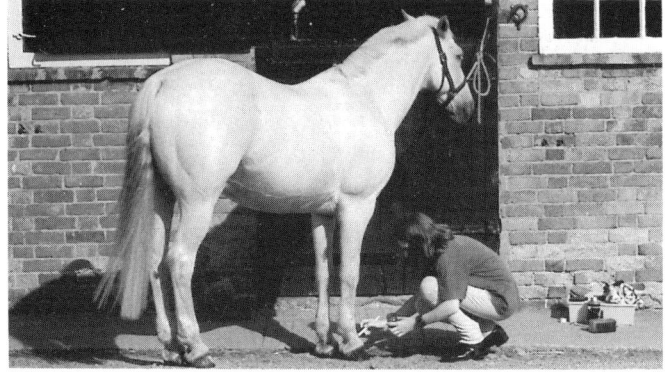

Start bandaging at the top, and place your left hand under the tail. Unroll about six inches of the bandage, and place this under the tail, holding it with your left hand, then bring the bandage over the tail, securing the end piece. This first part is the most difficult, and unless you make this secure the whole bandage will slip. Take the next turn above the first turn, and then bandage evenly down the tail to the end of the tail bone. Tie the tapes securely with a double bow, tucking in the ends neatly.

Finally, paint hoof oil on the hooves, being careful not to get it round the hair on the coronet. If your pony has white socks this will look awful, and hoof oil is bad for a pony's hair.

Washing

You should not wash your pony too often, but it is a useful way of getting him clean at the beginning of the Easter or summer school holidays, or before a show.

Use lukewarm water and a horse and pony shampoo, obtainable from the saddlers. It is not wise to use detergent; some ponies are very allergic to the harsh nature of detergents, and come out in rashes and blotches. Lather-up the shampoo well, wash the mane and tail, scrub the coat clean and then rinse with tepid water. Shake the tail around to get rid of excess water and then use a sweat scraper to get the excess water out of the coat.

Walk your pony around to dry him off.

If he is very hot after exercise, or competing, you can sponge or wash your pony. If he is rugged up it is important he does not get cold, and you must never put the rugs on him if he is damp. He will catch a chill. You can put on a sweat sheet (a light rug with many holes like an Aertex vest) underneath the jute rug which should go on upside down, so the inside will not get damp. Turn the rug the right way when he is completely dry.

You can put some straw underneath the sweat sheet to allow the air to circulate and dry him. Keep checking his ears; if they feel cold then your pony *is* cold and needs more rugs.

If your pony is stabled, clipped and very muddy after hunting, then you can wash him in the same manner as described provided it is not a very cold day. Pay special attention to the areas underneath his belly and girth. If mud is left here it can cause mud fever: the underneath becomes sore, raw and the skin flaky, causing the pony to become very sensitive. A pony's legs are also prone to mud fever. If your pony is stabled you can dry his legs by bandaging with straw underneath and then when dry brush out the mud.

If your pony is kept at grass then you must not wash him before or after hunting. Do not attempt to brush the wet mud after hunting; you will only make it look worse and it may cause mud fever. Make sure he is cool before you turn him out. If you turn out a warm, sweaty pony on a winter's night he will catch a chill. Healthy ponies will be perfectly all right out at grass after hunting, provided you feed them.

Shoeing

The care of the feet and shoeing are vital for your pony's welfare. We describe here the parts of the foot so you can understand why this is important, and how to care for your pony's feet. Most people refer to the man who shoes your horse as a blacksmith, but his real name is a farrier or shoeing smith.

Parts of the Foot

The line where the hard horn meets the flesh of the leg at the top of the foot is called the coronet. The horn, which makes up the outside of the hoof, is called the wall and this should be hard, without dents or rings. It should look healthy and strong, not flaky and brittle. The outer foot is not sensitive

KEEPING UP APPEARANCES

Parts of the Foot

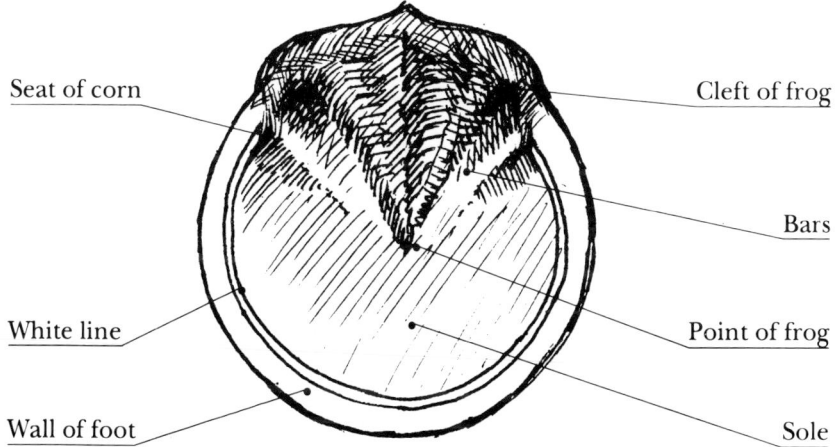

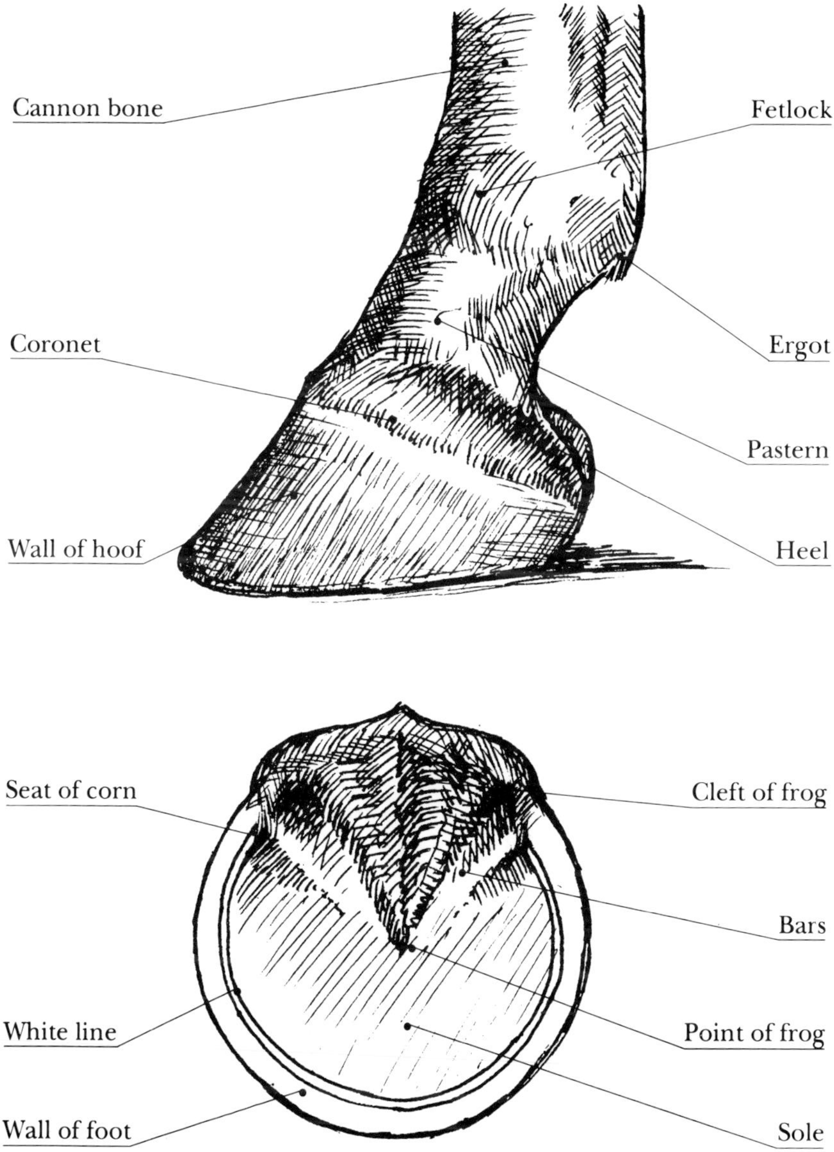

and it does not hurt your pony when he is shod, or has his feet cut back.

If you hold up your pony's foot you will see the

bottom of the wall which is called the sole, and ideally this should be nicely vaulted, not flat. The white line separates the wall from the sole. The triangular fleshy centre of the sole is the frog; this should be raised, not flat, acting as the shock absorber of the foot.

The frog should always be able to touch the ground, so your farrier will have to rasp away the wall of the foot as it grows. Some farriers do not cut away enough of the foot, and allow it to grow too long.

Your farrier should trim the foot before he fits new shoes. Your pony will need new shoes about every six weeks, depending on how much road work you have done. If the shoes are still in a good state, but the feet have grown long and the nails are coming loose, you can ask him to remove the shoes. This means taking off the shoes, cutting back and trimming the feet, and then putting on the same shoes again. Sometimes you can have a new set in front, and removals behind, depending on the wear; this will help your shoeing costs.

If you have difficulty in finding a good farrier, ask other Pony Club members to recommend one. It may be easier to take your pony to a friend's stable to be shod, as farriers are busy, and it is often difficult to get an appointment. A good farrier will be able to advise you if there are any irregularities in your pony's feet.

Most shoeing is now done cold, that is, the shoes are pre-shaped, and slightly adjusted to fit the pony's foot. Hot shoeing, where the shoes are heated to a high temperature to make them malleable so they can be hit to bend to the perfect shape of your pony's foot, is now very rare. A good farrier should make the shoe fit the pony's foot, not vice versa.

In between the farrier's visits you should check your pony's shoes. Run your hands over the wall of the foot; you should not be able to feel any risen nail clenches. If you do, it is a sign the shoe is working loose. You can temporarily improve it by hitting down the risen clenches with a hammer, but make an early appointment for a visit from your farrier.

If your pony loses a shoe during a ride, ideally you should dismount and lead the pony home. If your pony has strong feet and is not feeling too sore you can ride him quietly on the grass or verges. Sometimes, the shoe is half off, twisted with a nail sticking out. You will have to do your best, and try to pull it off. If your pony can walk without treading on the upturned nails, lead him quietly at a walk and the shoe may work loose. If the pony is treading on upturned nails, try to twist the shoe to improve it and get some help.

Care of the Foot

Apart from the attention to shoeing, you must pick your pony's feet out regularly. It is bad for him always to have packed mud and stones in his feet. This stops the frog working properly and prevents the air circulating to dry the foot. When the foot dries out any bacteria present are destroyed, thereby eliminating diseases of the feet, such as thrush. If your pony's feet begin to smell it is the first sign of ailments, so pay special attention to cleanliness.

Hoof oil protects the wall of the foot. If your pony's feet are brittle, Cornucrescene promotes growth and strengthens the horn.

Studs

If you are competing and jumping regularly, then you will probably decide your pony should wear studs in his shoes. These are metal protruding screw heads which stick into the ground to prevent your pony slipping. The shoe is made with a hole on the outer part. For normal exercising and daily wear, the hole is plugged with cotton wool to stop grit and dirt getting in. When you want to use studs, you then unplug the cotton wool, use a stud tap with metal thread at the bottom to wind round into the hole, and then screw up the stud. Your farrier will be able to advise you, and will have a supply of various studs.

You must not use the studs when riding on the road as your pony will not be able to move properly. They are best put in when you arrive at a show or event as you tack up. Never travel your pony in studs.

Clipping

Your pony will not need clipping to remove his winter coat, unless you intend to compete or hunt in the winter, or Easter holidays. Clipping your pony does mean that he will not sweat through the coat and become difficult to keep clean and tidy. It is also far more pleasant to ride a clipped pony.

However, this means your pony will require stabling, and more attention, which is a more expensive way of keeping him.

Different Types of Clipping

A full clip is known as a hunter clip. All the coat is clipped, except for the saddle patch and legs. These are left to give protection and prevent soreness. You should never clip your pony's heels. The growth of hair at the back of the heel prevents wetness and mud collecting in the heel area.

A trace clip is where the hair is removed from the tummy, shoulders and thighs up to the height at which the traces would run were the horse used for driving. You can also clip under the neck.

A blanket clip is where the hair is removed only from the neck and belly. If you imagine a blanket being left over a pony you will understand this.

Some horses' heads are clipped and then the hair

is left on the back. Racehorses are sometimes clipped in this way.

Clipping is a task for the experienced. It is important to have good clippers. You will probably find it easiest to ask someone to clip your pony for a reasonable charge: it works out cheaper than investing in clippers. You can also see how it is done, and start practising on the easiest areas first.

6 On The Right Tack

Saddlery, or tack, includes saddles, bridles, bits, martingales, breastplates and numnahs. It is vital equipment which you must choose carefully and maintain properly.

There is a huge variety of tack to suit various ponies and the tasks they are required to perform. Saddlery is expensive but necessary. It is important that it fits your pony well.

When you are buying a pony find out what tack it is used to as it is sensible to try this first of all. If the pony has performed well in a certain bit, martingale or noseband, it makes sense to continue. It may be possible to buy the tack with the pony.

You can buy saddlery second-hand, but make sure it is in good condition. Some second-hand tack is not safe, and may easily break during use. A snapped rein, stirrup leather, or girth can be highly dangerous while you are riding. One consolation in buying good-class saddlery is that it can be sold on for a fairly high price when you have outgrown your pony.

Saddles

There are on the market certain saddles which are imported and priced well below standard prices. These are generally inferior and should be avoided.

A good saddle should be comfortable, enabling the rider to sit in its centre. There are saddles for special purposes, such as dressage, show jumping

ON THE RIGHT TACK

and showing, but a general purpose saddle is the most suitable for young riders and can be used for all jumping and riding. Old-fashioned saddles cut very straight in front, are not suitable for modern riding instruction.

You should check that the saddle that you buy does not need restuffing. A saddle usually requires extra stuffing every couple of years, otherwise it gets too flat on the pony's back.

The main structure of a saddle is the tree (see diagram) which determines its shape. Saddle trees

Parts of the Saddle

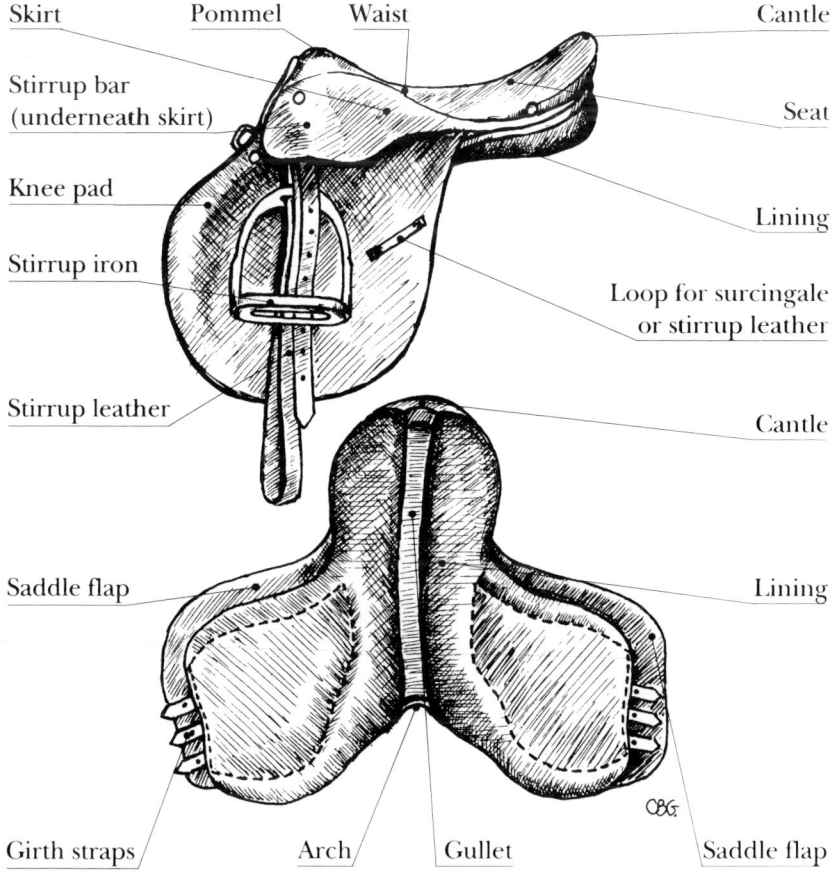

are made of plywood, plastic or fibreglass. The best is the spring tree variety which is flexible. Bands of webbing hold the stuffing on to the tree.

The stirrup bars are built on to the tree. These should always be left open and down, so the stirrup leather will pull off backwards if there is any danger of the rider being dragged with a foot in the stirrup.

There is a full, or half, panel underneath the saddle flap. Full panels are usually more expensive, but half panels are suitable for smaller ponies. The sweat flap protects the panels from the girth buckles, and the buckle guards protect the main saddle flap from the marks of the girth buckles.

Saddles can be lined with leather (which is costly, but long lasting), linen or serge. Serge takes a long time to dry and it is not used in manufacturing new saddles nowadays.

The saddle must fit your pony properly especially on the withers. You should be able to place your fingers under the pommel when you are riding and not get them pinched. This should also be true when the pony moves. A saddle may look as though it fits, but when there is weight in the seat, the pommel will come down further. A numnah or wither pad will protect the withers, but it is important there is enough room, or you will injure your pony's withers and make him reluctant to move forward as he will be in pain.

There should be a clear gully under the centre of the saddle from front to back. If you get yourself into a position either in front or behind the saddle you should be able to look underneath and see this.

The saddle should not go too far back on to the loins of the pony, hurting his back. One often sees young riders with saddles far too big for their ponies.

If a saddle tends to move forward, especially on a small pony with a low wither, you will need a crupper which goes around the tail and attaches to the back of the saddle.

If your pony is rather flat sided, the girths and saddle may tend to slip backwards, so you will need a breastplate which goes around the neck and on to the front of the saddle at both sides. Some ponies are ridden with breastplates anyway because they are required to jump when competing or hunting.

Stirrup Leathers and Irons

Stirrup leathers can be made of ordinary leather or rawhide. Leather does not last as long as rawhide, and can break when dried out. It is important to keep leathers well oiled. The rawhide variety are almost unbreakable, but they do stretch, so adjustment is required or you will find yourself riding too long. If you intend to compete or hunt, it is best to invest in the rawhide variety, but for showing the leather sort is smarter and neater.

Stirrup irons should be made of good quality metal or they will bend. Never use nickel stirrup irons as they can bend, causing accidents. It is most important that your foot is not too tight in the stirrup iron or you may be dragged if you fall off. There should be half an inch free at each side of the widest part of the foot. If there is more than this there is the danger that your foot will slip through. Children should not ride in their younger brothers' or sisters' stirrups as they are unlikely to fit properly. It is dangerous to ride in anything other than a proper riding or jodhpur boot. Some sturdy walking shoes are safe, but it is important you have a heel to prevent your foot slipping through. Please remember that wellington boots and trainers are dangerous for riding in.

Rubber stirrup treads can be used in stirrups to help grip, and these also help to keep your feet warm in winter.

Safety Stirrups

These have a rubber band replacing the metal on the outside, thus there is no danger of a foot being trapped in the stirrup as the rubber band is designed to come off or break if necessary. However, you must adjust the band so that it does not come off too easily. These are mainly suitable for young children learning to ride. Once a child can ride and balance the foot in the stirrup properly it is best to progress to ordinary stirrups.

Bridles And Bits

Most ponies are ridden in snaffle bridles. Only an experienced rider should attempt to ride with a double bridle, and then, after expert tuition. Except for advanced showing, double bridles are not necessary for ponies, and most work much better in snaffles. When judging, I often see a pony which would be much better in a snaffle as the rider is just not experienced enough to manage a double bridle.

The headpiece and the throat lash are made from the same piece of leather. The throat lash is designed to do up on the near side of the pony, and the headpieces attach to the cheekstraps, which in turn support the bit in the mouth. The browband comes in front of the pony's ears and stops the headpiece slipping back. (See illustration).

The reins have a central buckle and are usually made of leather. To make them easier to grip they may be plaited or laced leather, or plaited nylon, or have a rubber grip covering over leather.

The most popular reins nowadays are the rubber grip ones as they do not slip when wet. The leather variety are generally used for showing, and the plaited nylon for small ponies.

There are different types of noseband, but the simplest is the plain cavesson noseband. This is the only noseband to which a standard martingale can be attached. A drop noseband may be worn to stop

ON THE RIGHT TACK

Parts of the Bridle

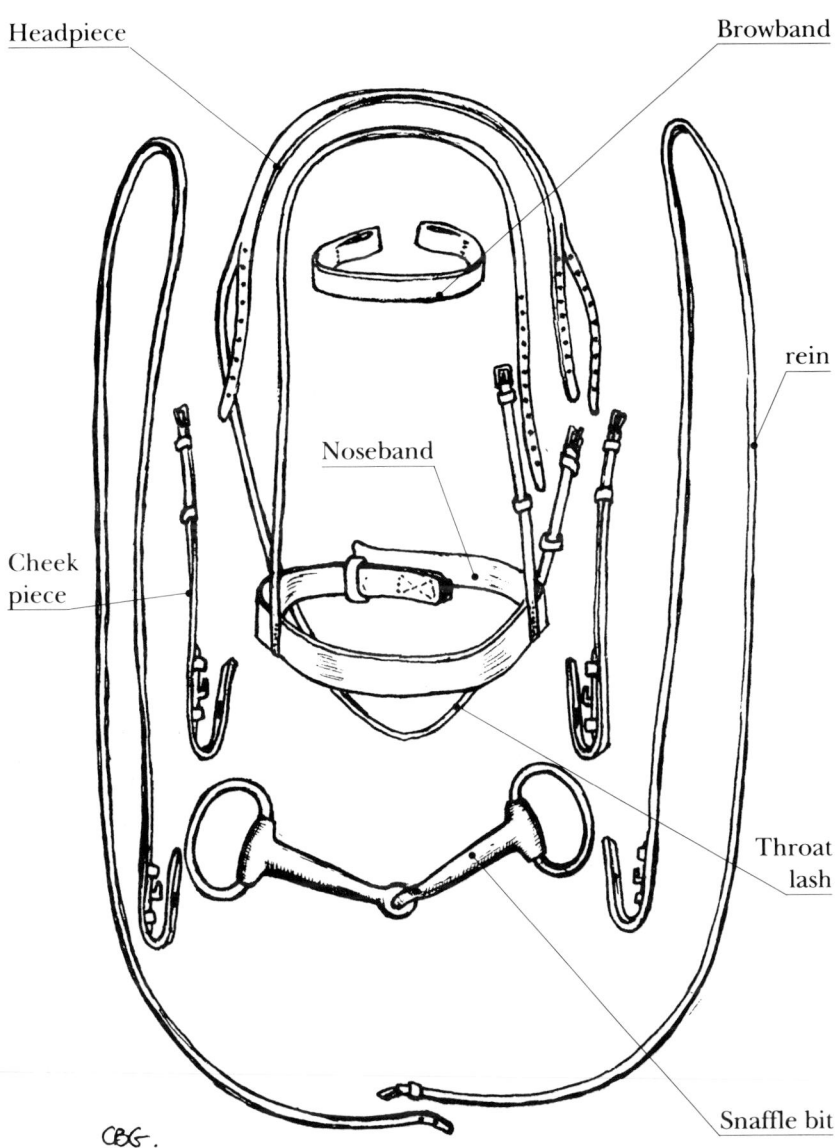

the pony opening its mouth, or crossing its jaw in an attempt to avoid the bit. We discuss the use of drop nosebands and their fitting later in this chapter.

YOUR PONY

Assembling the Bridle

Types of bit: clockwise from bottom left: eggbutt jointed snaffle, mouthing bit with keys (used for breaking in), vulcanite plain-bar snaffle, kimblewick with curb chain, leather curb chain, vulcanite pelham, straight-bar pelham, twisted snaffle, ringed jointed snaffle.

It is always easiest to start with the headpiece, and thread the browband on so that the throat lash is at the back. Hang the headpiece on a hook so that you do not get in a muddle, and then in attaching the billets, thread through the keepers first then slide them backwards and attach the cheekstraps. Next thread the noseband and headpiece strap underneath the bridle headpiece, through the browband, and do up the noseband headpiece. Attach the bit, making sure that it will be the correct way up when in the horse's mouth, and then attach the reins.

To hang up your bridle properly you should thread the reins in the throat lash so they do not trail on the floor, and then do the noseband up around the bridle, but do not do the buckle up, just slide it through the keepers.

A double bridle comprises a bridoon, which is a snaffle, but smaller than an ordinary snaffle, plus a curb bit, together with a curb chain and lip strap. The bridoon acts in the same manner as an ordinary snaffle and the curb acts to give more collection and inflection. The curb, in effect, greatly increases the

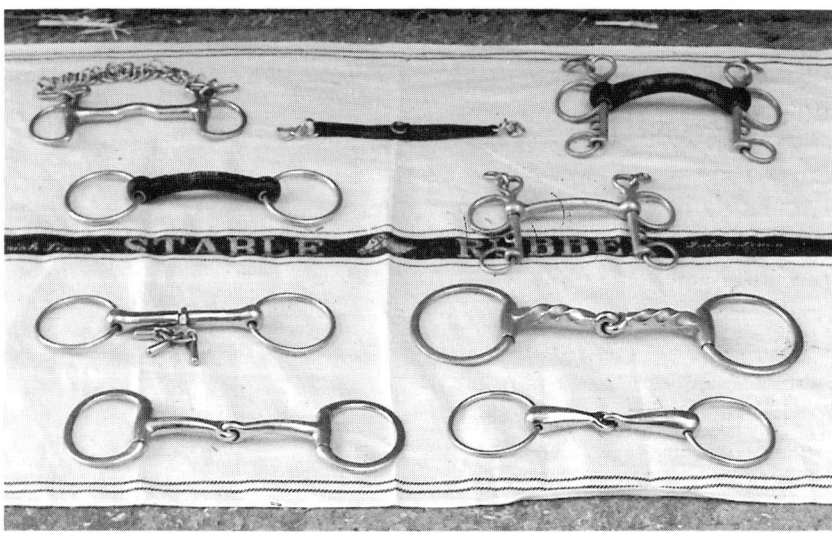

pressure on the mouth through the leverage of the straight piece projecting down, known as the port, to which the curb rein is attached.

Bits

The bits used with a snaffle bridle can vary. A jointed snaffle or a pelham are the most widely used. They are attached to the cheekstraps by hooked billets, or stitched for showing which looks neater. Sometimes hooked billets can be difficult to undo, and the knack is to put your thumb and forefinger between the bit and billet on either side, gently lift up, and at the same time push the piece of leather on the top with your thumb.

Snaffles

Snaffles are either jointed, giving a 'nutcracker' effect, or a straight mouthpiece, acting on the corners of the lips and the bars of the mouth. It is not a strong bit, and makes the pony raise its head. The jointed snaffle is the most common, and there are various forms of this. The egg butt snaffle has fixed rings which are egg shaped where they join the mouthpiece to prevent pinching. The twisted snaffle is more severe; and the straight cheekstrap snaffle prevents the bit from turning in the pony's mouth, being generally used for smaller ponies.

The straight bar snaffles are milder than the jointed type and some are made of vulcanite or rubber to be even softer. A rubber snaffle is the softest bit there is, and may be used for a pony which has had its mouth spoilt by rough hands.

The curb has extending cheekstraps, and a curb chain underneath the chin. This gives a levering action when the rein is applied. The action of the bit in the mouth, and poll pressure from the headpiece of the bridle cause the pony to drop his head and bend his neck.

The pelham bit combines the action of the snaffle

and curb. It suits some ponies who are too strong for a snaffle, and it suits children, for whom two reins can be complicated as the pelham can be used with a single rein. The pelham is used with a curb chain and lip strap.

The Kimblewick is a good bit for strong ponies as it is a curb, affording more control than a snaffle. It has an unjointed mouthpiece and a curb chain. Its advantage is that it is used with a single rein and it is easy to handle.

It is important that the bit is the correct width for your pony's mouth. If too narrow it will pinch him, and if too wide it will move from side to side and not have the correct action. Most ponies will go well in either a snaffle or Kimblewick, but there are many other types of bits and bridles, including gags, which are severe, to deal with headpullers, and hackamores (bitless bridles), which are usually used on horses and ponies whose mouths have been spoilt by hard handling.

Nosebands

Apart from the cavesson noseband, there are drop nosebands, flash nosebands and grackle nosebands, all variations designed to stop your pony opening his mouth. These nosebands should be carefully fitted to avoid interfering with the breathing. If your pony needs a drop noseband then you should seek expert help with the fitting. It is important to have the cheekstraps relatively high, and the strap below the bit tight enough so that it does not come off.

Martingales

The standing martingale is a strap from the back of the cavesson noseband down between the forelegs to the girth, held in place by a neck strap. It is used to prevent your pony from throwing his head up.

The correct length of the standing martingale strap should be determined by passing the strap from the cross right up to the pony's junction of head and neck. Shorten or lengthen the strap accordingly, using the buckle provided, and then attach the loop to the noseband.

Much more frequently used nowadays is the running martingale. It is the same as a standing martingale, except that the end is divided in two and attached to each rein with a ring, allowing it to slide freely. It is important to make sure the rings are facing the correct way and not twisted. The purpose of a running martingale is to improve control of a horse or pony which throws its head about frequently, but it has become almost standard nowadays whether the animal needs it or not. Riders like it because it provides a neck strap to hold on to at crucial moments.

An Irish martingale is not generally used for ponies. It is a short strap with a ring on each end, threaded on to the reins. It is employed to prevent horses throwing the reins over their heads and is mainly used for racehorses.

Looking after Saddlery

Saddlery can easily be damaged by careless handling.

Never throw your saddle down as it may be crushed or torn. A saddle should always be put on a rack, or put against a wall or support. Stand it upright on its pommel, as this avoids damage to the tree. It is better to lean your saddle against a wall or fence than put it over the stable door or gate as it is easy for your pony to push it off on to the ground. To avoid scratching the pommel and cantle, you can fold the girth over the back.

Saddles are easiest carried over your arm or against your side with the pommel downwards. You should run the stirrups up so they do not hit you around the legs as you walk.

Try and get into the habit of putting your saddlery in safe places where it will not get knocked about as you are grooming your pony. If you drop the saddle or if it is badly damaged the tree may be broken. It is not unknown for cars to run over saddles. Some saddles can never be repaired and for those that can it is very costly.

If you have to leave your pony in his stable after tacking up always tie him up, so that he does not roll and damage the saddle tree.

You should treat your bridle with equal care. Try to avoid throwing it on the ground, and get into the habit of looping the reins and martingale if you have one, in the throat lash every time you take it off. This does not take any extra time and saves you unravelling all the twisted reins next time you want it. It is foolish to use reins to tether horses and ponies; the reins quickly get broken. Put a head collar on over the bridle and tether your pony with the head-collar rope.

Tack Cleaning

You may well find tack cleaning an absolute bore. It is even worse if you have to be told that you cannot have supper until you have cleaned your saddle. Some children only give a thought to tack cleaning just before a big show, or when it may be inspected by their Pony Club instructor.

Unless tack is cleaned properly and regularly it will never be supple, nor look smart. More important, it will not last long, and you will find you have to replace it. Hard and dirty saddlery may rub and chafe sensitive parts of your pony.

Whenever you ride your tack should be cleaned afterwards, or at least wiped over to remove dirt and sweat. All your saddlery should be taken to pieces to clean it thoroughly.

Daily Tack Cleaning
You will need :
A sponge for washing, and a towelling cloth for drying.
Another sponge or piece of foam rubber for putting on saddle soap.
Saddle soap, either in a tin or a bar.
Neatsfoot oil.
Metal polish and cloth.
A stiff brush for removing sweat from any webbing girths or serge linings.
Bucket of tepid (just warm) water.

Wipe over or wash leather if muddy to remove all dirt and grease. If you wash, then dry over with the cloth. Put on saddle soap freely with the sponge used especially for this purpose. Keep the sponge as dry as possible, and rub saddle soap well into all parts of the leather.

If you use the bar saddle soap, dip the end of the bar in the bucket of water and rub it on the sponge. If you use the tin, put the damp sponge in the tin, but do not get the soap too wet. It is not necessary to work up a lather.

At least weekly you should take your bridle to pieces, clean all the buckles, and use neatsfoot oil to keep it supple.

You should use neatsfoot oil more often in the winter if your tack has been wet, to replace the natural oils. Put the oil mainly on the underside with a sponge or a paint brush you keep especially for this. After it has been absorbed, apply saddle soap.

Never use anything else to clean leather. Normal bath soap, detergents, washing powder or bleach will ruin saddlery. Saddlery should be dried naturally or in winter in gentle warmth. Never put tack to dry in front of the fire or by a radiator: leather must not dry out too quickly as it will crack.

Method Of Cleaning

Saddle

Remove the girths, girth-guards, stirrup leathers and detach the stirrup irons. Put the irons in the bucket of water to soak.

Thoroughly clean all the leather work with tepid water, but do not make your saddle too wet. Soap all areas especially under the flaps. Do not use too much saddle soap on the seat, and *never* apply neatsfoot oil to the seat area.

Some saddles have suede knee rolls, and these should just be brushed clean. Do not apply soap nor oil to suede.

Next clean all metal work with metal polish.

If your saddle lining is of leather, it can be cleaned the same as the other leather, making sure you have first removed all traces of dirt and sweat. You can use a blunt knife if this is difficult. For linen linings sponge off or scrub, but keep the lining as dry as possible.

Wipe over the irons, and rubber treads if you use them and apply metal polish to the irons. Clean stirrup leathers and girths with saddle soap. It is easier to hang these from a hook and pull on them to clean. You may find it difficult to put the stirrup leathers back on the stirrup bars. They are designed so they do not come off backwards too easily. The knack here is to raise the cantle while holding the pommel steady and then they will slip in. At first, you may need another person to raise the cantle for you.

Leather girths should be treated with neatsfoot regularly as they dry out with sweat and wet, muddy conditions. Nylon or webbing girths should be brushed or washed.

Numnahs

There are many varieties on the market nowadays. Some thin numnahs can be washed in the washing machine, but others are not washable so follow the manufacturer's instructions taking care to rinse the soap out thoroughly. It is important to clean your numnah regularly; if it becomes hard it can give your pony a sore back and may make him unrideable.

Bridle
At first, you may find it difficult to put your bridle together after cleaning with saddle soap as described above, but practice does make perfect. Undo all the buckles and take it apart. You may find it helpful to put the pieces in some sort of order, so you can remember how to do it up again.

Put the bit into the bucket of water to soak. Wash or wipe over the different parts of the bridle. Leather reins should be supple, but do not use too much soap as they will become slippery. Rubber and string reins should just be wiped over.

Martingales, breastplates and neck straps are cleaned in the same way as the bridle. You will find it easier to hang up the pieces on hooks, and the same applies to stirrup leathers and the girth. Make sure you remove all the dirt and grease before saddle soaping.

Rugs
Your grass-kept pony should not need a rug of any kind. Even in winter a healthy pony will not need a New Zealand rug. It is detrimental for him to wear one as it stops growth of the coat, and causes rubbing if left on all the time.

A stabled pony not clipped, or just trace clipped, only needs a New Zealand rug when it is very cold and he spends a long day outside.

A fully clipped pony will need a jute rug and blankets depending on the temperature.

New Zealand Rug
The New Zealand rug is made of a green waterproof

canvas with a woollen lining. It can have either a fixed surcingale (a strap running over the saddle area and underneath to keep the rug in place), or one that is slotted through the sides of the rug.

There are usually two straps at the chest and two straps encircling the hind legs which cross over.

The New Zealand rug needs to fit your pony well, as it will rub or slip if badly fitted. You should never keep the rug on permanently. It should be removed part of each day to allow air to circulate around the coat.

Most ponies are well used to New Zealand rugs, but the first time you put it on be wary, as it can be frightening until your pony is used to it. Just put it

ON THE RIGHT TACK

on and off a few times for a day or two, and lead your pony around the yard in it.

Jute Rug (Night Rug)

Made of jute with a woollen lining, this rug is worn with extra blankets by clipped ponies. During the day your pony can wear only the jute rug, but you must adjust the blankets, depending on the weather. Put on a blanket or two if cold. A pony that is cold will never look in good condition. He will always look 'tucked up'.

You can check whether he is warm enough by feeling his ears. If they feel cold then your pony feels cold all over.

Rugs are kept in position with a surcingale which is sometimes attached to the rug or a roller. A roller is a surcingale which is padded across the back to protect the back bones. The blanket is folded back underneath the roller to keep it secure. It is important to ensure the blanket is well forward, as you will find it will tend to slip backwards. Ponies can tear blankets and rugs if they tread over them in the night.

Day Rug

These are smart coloured woollen rugs with bindings. They are used generally for special occasions when your pony needs to be warm. They can be used at shows or hunter trials or for travelling. They tend to become spoilt if used for ordinary stable use.

Summer Sheet

These are checked heavy cotton rugs which can be used in the summer to keep a pony's coat clean for showing. These do not keep your pony warm.

Anti-Sweat Sheet

This looks like a large coloured string vest. It is used after strenuous riding, and lets air reach the pony's body to cool him while keeping him warm. This is essential to use under a jute rug inside when your pony is hot. You can put your pony's jute rug on him inside out until he is dry, so the woollen lining does not become damp. Your pony can easily catch a chill if allowed to become cold after exercise.

Cleaning Rugs

Rugs are cleaned by spreading them out in the yard and scrubbing them with washing powder. They must be rinsed or hosed off and take ages to dry. Hang them over a gate or fence.

They should be cleaned at the end of winter when not required so they are packed away clean. Some summer sheets and anti-sweat rugs can be put in the washing machine, but if they have leather straps, they should be washed by hand.

Brushing Boots

Ponies do not really need boots, but if you compete and jump regularly, they do protect your pony's legs from any bangs, particularly from self-inflicted wounds. He may, for example, injure himself by 'over reaching', striking the back of a foreleg with the metal-shod toe of a hind leg.

Brushing boots are of leather, or felt and leather, and strapped around the leg, usually nowadays with Velcro fastenings which are easy for young riders to fasten.

Over-reach boots are rubber boots worn specifically to protect the back foot striking into the back of the front heel or tendons.

Tail Guard

Worn to protect a pony's tail if he is in the habit of rubbing it when travelling. The tail is fastened up on to the roller, put on outside a tail bandage.

Poll Guard

A padded protection for some ponies who raise their heads too high or plunge while travelling. They are mainly used for large horses whose heads are up near the ceiling of trailers or horse boxes. Ponies seldom need them.

7 Looking Good

If you are interested in riding seriously you will begin to collect a complete riding kit. For occasional weekend riders a hard hat, jodhpur boots and jodhpurs are the only essential items to buy. New riding clothes can be expensive, but even old clothes can be perfectly presentable if well fitting, cleaned, pressed and correctly worn.

Hard Hats

The Pony Club rightly insists on all its members wearing approved safety headgear. Even if you are not a member you should do the same.

Falling off a pony is increasingly dangerous because there are so many more hard surfaces to land on in the modern world. Never ride hatless; always wear either a skull cap or a riding hat bearing the British Safety Institute kite mark and a BSI number.

The Pony Club insists that all members wear skull caps up to BSI 4472 standard. The present BSI standard number for riding hats is 3686. Look for these numbers in the manufacturer's label.

The riding hat and the skull cap each has a fibre glass dome, and shock absorbing plastic insulation inside. They are secured by a chinstrap and harness at the back designed to stop them slipping on impact.

The riding hat has a flexible peak, so that on striking the ground it bends and reduces the impact if you fall on your face. Over the skull cap you can wear a velvet or silk covering, with a flexible peak, in blue or black. Wearing a safe, modern hat with a chinstrap is not a sissy thing to do. Jockeys, horse trials riders and show jumpers wear them nowadays. Head injuries are so serious that you must do everything possible to lessen the risk. So do not try to save money by buying a cheap riding hat which is not up to BSI standard. Wear the skull cap or safety hat at *all* times when riding your pony.

Body Protectors

The Pony Club nowadays insist on members wearing body protectors for cross-country riding in events or hunter trials. It is well worth wearing them at all times – certainly whenever you are jumping, whether schooling or competing. There is a good range of slim fitting protectors, worn like a jacket which will fit under a sweater or a tweed coat.

The protector will greatly reduce the risk of broken ribs or, much worse, injury to your spine. Get into the habit of wearing one. Like the safety hat, it is *not* sissy. Sensible but daring riders, such as professional jockeys, always wear them.

Jodhpurs

These are close fitting and made of a stretch material so you can move easily.

They are usually beige or off-white, but nowadays can be found in a range of other colours. If you are going to ride often you may find it best to keep a beige pair for best, and to buy a navy blue pair for every day use. Navy or black jodhpurs are becoming more popular as they are more practical. There are also jodhpurs made of denim. It is usually uncomfortable to ride in jeans: they tend to rub, pinch and chafe.

If your jodhpurs ride up you can buy a jodhpur clip to attach them under your boots. Second-hand jodhpurs are a good buy, especially for young children as they are often outgrown while still fairly new.

Breeches (pronounced 'britches') are exactly the same as jodhpurs, but shorter as they are designed to be worn with riding boots.

Jodhpur Boots

These are short black or brown leather ankle boots with elastic inserts so that you can get them on. Sometimes they have ankle straps around the tops, instead of elastic.

They have become part of a fashion trend and you will see them for sale in shoe shops. The fashion varieties are not suitable for riding as they do not have a proper heel and they will allow your heel to slide through the stirrup. This would be dangerous, and for the same reason it is unsafe to ride in Wellington boots or trainers.

Again, you can often find second-hand jodhpur boots, particularly in small sizes.

Some jodhpur boots are now being made in rubber which are easier to wash off and dry when muddy. Leather jodhpur boots must be properly cleaned and polished with shoe polish. They will not last if they are left wet and muddy, as they will soon crack.

Knee-length riding boots are mainly for older teenage riders; these boots are also available in leather or rubber. When you start hunting seriously, and your feet have stopped growing, it is best to invest in proper leather riding boots. They will protect your legs better if you hit a gatepost or get kicked by other riders' horses. Riding boots can be black or brown for teenagers, but if you wear a black coat you should wear black boots.

Rubber riding boots are useful if you hack out in the winter when it is muddy. You can wear them as well for all stable management; otherwise you will need a non-slip pair of Wellingtons.

Many children wear rubber riding boots for hunting, and they will save your lower leg from getting muddy and wet. Some makes are lined and offer better leg protection. However, they do get hot in summer.

Jackets And Jumpers

For hacking and riding-school lessons you can wear a shirt, jumper or modern sweatshirt. If it is cold enough, you can add an anorak, parka or waxed jacket.

Plain clothes are more practical and look best for riding. You should avoid very bright colours; they do not look workmanlike and will not be practical. It is easy to stain clothes permanently when riding or working with ponies.

If you are keen, and decide to ride regularly and compete in shows and hunter trials, or go hunting, you should try to invest in a hacking jacket: a tweed jacket which is waisted, with one slit at the back. This is the correct dress for hunting, hacking, showing and rallies. You may be lucky and find a good second-hand one.

It is important that your hacking jacket fits properly. You may have to try on several before deciding. If you are still growing it should allow for growth. You can turn the sleeves up and alter the buttons so there is more overlap. It should not be too short; it must cover the hips and upper thigh.

We often see young riders with badly fitting hacking jackets; far too tight, or hanging off them. Once you find one with a good shape and fit for you, minor alterations may have to be made to narrow the width of the shoulders or the back. It is always better to take in; letting out is nearly impossible. Your local dry cleaners may be able to carry out alterations; it is a task for a tailor not a novice dressmaker.

YOUR PONY

As we have recommended, you should wear your body protector whenever you ride, so try your hacking jacket on with one underneath. A black or navy blue jacket is necessary for classes at larger shows, or for older teenagers when hunting.

Shirt And Tie

Any plain, light coloured shirt can be worn and if you are a member of the Pony Club, wear the official tie. If not, do wear a plain tie in the hunting field and at shows.

Hunting Tie

With a hacking jacket you can wear a spotted hunting tie for hunting and hunter trialling. If you wear a black jacket hunting you then wear a white stock. A hunting tie, sometimes incorrectly called a 'stock', must be tied correctly (see diagram).

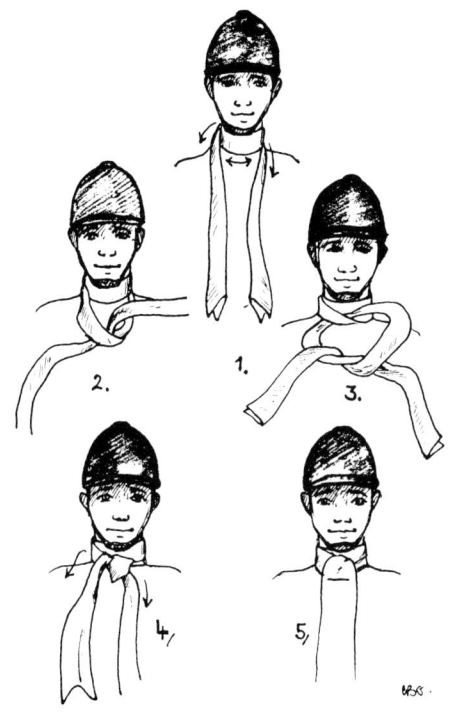

Gloves

There are many varieties of gloves on the market for riding. Ordinary gloves are not suitable for riding: you will find they are either too bulky, too thin and will go into holes or they do not grip the reins well. For correct wear, cream or pale yellow string gloves are best but the rubber-backed variety are good for everyday wear. Leather gloves are expensive and only used for showing.

Riding Mac

The long waxed, or PVC riding mac can of course be useful but you can improvise with your anorak and waterproof leggings. Ordinary mackintoshs are not suitable for riding as they are not adapted for sitting on a pony!

Cross-Country Colours

For cross-country competitive riding it is fun to wear colours similar to those worn by jockeys. This is a striped or patterned top in a shirt style, but with only a few top buttons, with either a plain or matching skull cover in silk. Some hunter trials specify that you should wear hunting clothes, so check up first.

Whips

A general purpose cutting whip is sufficient for most riding. Do not choose the long cutting whip, which is used for dressage or schooling by experienced riders. A hunting whip with a handle is ideal for hunting for those riders who are confident with their ponies. (See Chapter 12 on hunting.)

8 *Fit For Anything*

You need to understand when your pony is in good health and condition before you are able to notice disorders. It is best if you can spot health problems as soon as they appear.

A pony that is well and in good condition should be alert and interested, with a glossy coat. His eyes should be bright, and he should be breathing normally.

Most ponies are sound and they look after themselves very well. Our native breeds have been tough and hardy for generations, and this is passed on to our riding ponies today.

We have stressed the importance of regularly checking your pony, at least once a day when he is at grass and several times a day if stabled.

Most of the ailments and disorders we mention we hope you may never come across, but you should have a knowledge of what is involved.

Unless an ailment is slight, you should call your vet. Keep his telephone number handy. It is always best to telephone early in the morning before your vet plans his day, and give him as much notice as possible that you need a visit.

Try to notice as many symptoms about your pony as you can, so that you can give an exact description over the telephone to the vet.

If you are worried, you can telephone your vet to ask his advice, and he can decide whether it is necessary to see the pony.

When a pony becomes ill, it can happen quickly,

FIT FOR ANYTHING

sometimes within hours, and it is important to realize when your pony is not normal, and when to call for expert advice. Here are some signs to look for when checking your pony.

A pony is seriously ill if it is unable to get up and move freely, is bleeding badly or cannot put its foot to the ground easily. These conditions need urgent veterinary help. A pony should not be sweating at rest except in very hot weather. It is a sign of pain if the pony is sweating at rest, and sometimes a pony in distress will grind his teeth as well.

If your pony is lying down you must encourage him to get up, sometimes by a slap or prod to his quarters if he is lazy. Stand well clear when he does get up. If he is uncomfortable and unwilling to get up or keeps looking at his flanks he may have colic, a severe obstruction in the intestines. You should get him into a stable, call the vet and keep the pony moving gently until the vet arrives.

If your pony has an accident while out riding and blood is pumping out of a wound quickly tie a scarf or handkerchief round it with as much pressure as possible. You may have to use your hand as well. You should call for help from a friend immediately and get the vet to come as soon as you can. Try not to move the pony too far, or you will start the bleeding again. If the blood keeps flowing it may mean that an artery or vein is severed. Do not panic; a pony can lose a great deal of blood without much harm.

Lesser cuts and wounds may require stitching and antibiotics, so bring your pony into a stable and wash the wound thoroughly and keep it clean. Bleeding will cease in due course. Try to provide some hot water for the vet when he arrives.

If a pony has to be stitched he should be kept in for a few days to keep the dressing and wound clean and dry. Your vet will explain how to treat the wound. Your pony will also require antibiotics given by your vet to guard against infection.

Laminitis

This is a serious, and all too common, cause of lameness in ponies, and one which all pony owners should guard against. It is known as 'fever in the feet' and is caused by an excessive rich diet and lack of exercise. We have discussed this in the chapter on grazing (Chapter 3).

A pony with this condition is reluctant to move and becomes rooted to the spot. Laminitis always affects all four feet. You should carefully observe your pony in the spring months when the grass is lush. If he is getting too fat, forming a crest in his mane and seems to 'potter' on his feet, then restrict his diet. Once a pony has had laminitis he is prone to it for life. In severe cases the horn of the feet become ringed, so you can tell if a pony has suffered before.

The treatment your vet will prescribe is to limit the diet and to lunge the pony regularly. You cannot ride the pony, but although it will be painful for your pony to move at first, lunging will gradually improve him as it gives him good exercise. Surgical shoeing with flattened shoes may be necessary.

You may feel you are being harsh with your pony, but to cure laminitis you have to be 'cruel' to be kind. Otherwise laminitis becomes incurable, and you may have to put your pony down.

Worming

Red worms and round worms are common in ponies if they are not regularly treated. We have described how the native ponies are very susceptible to worm infestations which spoil their condition. If you do not worm ponies regularly every six to eight weeks, then the pasture becomes worm ridden and the pony will continually be subject to parasitic infestation. Your pony will never look well if he has worms.

It is easy to worm your pony. Vets and saddlers sell worm powders which can be put into the feed. If your pony is a fussy feeder you may have to give a worm paste orally; it is sold with a plastic plunger which you insert into the mouth. This is not as difficult as it sounds.

Skin Disorders
Lice And Mange
Skin parasites cause a general loss of condition and of course affect the coat. Dirty ponies can catch lice, and they will not disappear until treated with lice powder.

Ringworm
An extremely infectious skin disorder which causes bald ring patches. Your vet will recommend treatment either in the feed or in the form of a wash. You should avoid grooming the pony and thereby spreading ringworm through the tack. Ringworm is contagious to humans so be careful you are scrupulously clean after seeing your pony. It is sometimes caught by ponies turned out in fields with cattle.

Sweet Itch
Many ponies suffer from this unsightly and irritating skin condition on the crest, withers, croup and tail region. It will cause a pony to rub these parts raw. It occurs in early summer and is due to midge bites. Stabling will improve the condition and there is now a course of injections to help ponies become immunized. Some ponies suffering from sweet itch have their manes hogged.

Swellings
Swellings are abnormal. On the body they can be caused by an abscess: a pus-filled infection; melanomas: a cancerous growth; strangles: contagious infectious disease with symptoms of swellings under the throat; or warble flies which cause lumps on the saddle area. Allergies and stings will also cause minor swellings.

Swellings on the legs can be caused by fractures, splints, sprained tendons and ligaments, abscesses (which need animal lintex poulticing), ringbones and sidebones, sesamoiditis (filled legs through jarring spavins), curbs on hocks, throughpins, or capped hocks. Some conditions do not cause lameness or may be old injuries. Your vet will be able to advise. If your pony has always had a swelling, and been sound then you have no need to worry unless it gets worse. It is important to notice new swellings.

Heat

In the feet or legs this can indicate a sprain, soreness or jarring. It is usually accompanied by a swelling although this may only be slight. Heat on the legs or body may indicate infection.

Irregular or Excessive Breathing

Heavy breathing is a serious symptom with ill ponies, but it can also be caused by an allergy to hay and dust. You will find your pony coughs, and if you remove the cause – all the hay and straw – and use shavings or shredded paper bedding, his breathing will improve.

Coughing

Coughing is mainly linked to irregular breathing and can be the cause of colds and pneumonia, equine 'flu or an allergy. Lung worm can also cause coughing.

Discharge from the Nostrils

A discharge from one or both nostrils is abnormal and may mean your pony has a chill, equine 'flu, strangles or pneumonia. Feel his ears and if they are very cold it means your pony is cold throughout. You should get him into a stable and rug him up. Take his temperature if you can (see later this chapter), and if it is raised you will have to call the vet.

Bleeding from the Nostrils

This is rare in ponies and indicates a burst blood vessel. It generally occurs during exertion and you will have to stop and quieten your pony until the bleeding stops. You should then seek veterinary advice. It may be associated with anaemia and a change of diet and vitamin injection could be necessary.

Lameness

When a pony is in pain it becomes lame. The lameness can be caused by a disorder mostly of the foot, but also the pastern, fetlock, cannon bones, tendons and ligaments, knees or shoulder and stifles.

Lameness is sometimes complex and even experts and vets disagree on the causes and treatment. It can be serious, causing the pony to be unable to put his foot to the ground, or very minor. For instance, after a day's jumping on hard ground at a show your pony may go slightly 'short' and recover the next day. This should be a warning to you and you should rest the pony from jarring on hard ground, or worse leg troubles will occur.

We have stressed that you must call the vet urgently if your pony cannot put his foot to the ground. This is always serious. He may have something trapped in his foot which will require poulticing, and he will need antibiotics to guard against infection.

For other lameness you should ascertain which leg is painful. This is not as easy as it sounds. Ask someone to trot him up for you. More pressure will be put on one leg than the other.

The lame leg is the one receiving the least weight, and generally the least active one.

If your pony stands with one front foot in front of the other, and unbalanced, it usually means he has something wrong with his foot. However, do not worry if he rests his hind leg. This is normal, but make sure he will put proper weight on it if you move him over.

Any swelling or heat in the legs or joints is not normal. You should become accustomed to comparing your pony's legs as a pair to notice any differences.

Your vet will find it helpful if you tell him recent activities of your pony, and the date he was last shod. He may ask for a farrier to be present when he visits or for the shoes to be taken off before.

Here we list some of the most common lamenesses and disorders associated with ponies:

Sprains

Tendons and ligaments can be injured or inflamed after hard work, a sudden wrench, competing, or hunting on difficult going. There will be heat, and the affected area will be swollen. You will have to rest your pony and put on cold-water bandages.

Ponies very rarely sprain tendons, suspensory or check ligaments, but these cause severe lameness.

Broken Knees

Wounds and broken skin caused by the pony falling on to his knees. This is nasty immediately after it has occurred, but if proper veterinary treatment is given, possibly with stitching, and infection is avoided, then the wounds can recover well. You can always see bare patches at the site of the wound, and if the bone is damaged there will be permanent swellings.

Overreach

An overreach is a gash or blow to the back of the leg or heel of a front leg caused by the shoe of the hind leg. It is due to the action and length of stride of the pony. Ponies that have overreached are likely to do this again, and it is best to put on brushing boots so that the overreach does not cut through the skin of the back of the cannon bones harming the tendons. Overreach boots can also be worn to protect the back of the heel. Your farrier can alter the shoeing by putting quarter clips on the hind shoes and setting the hind shoes back

Parts of the Foreleg Liable to Injury

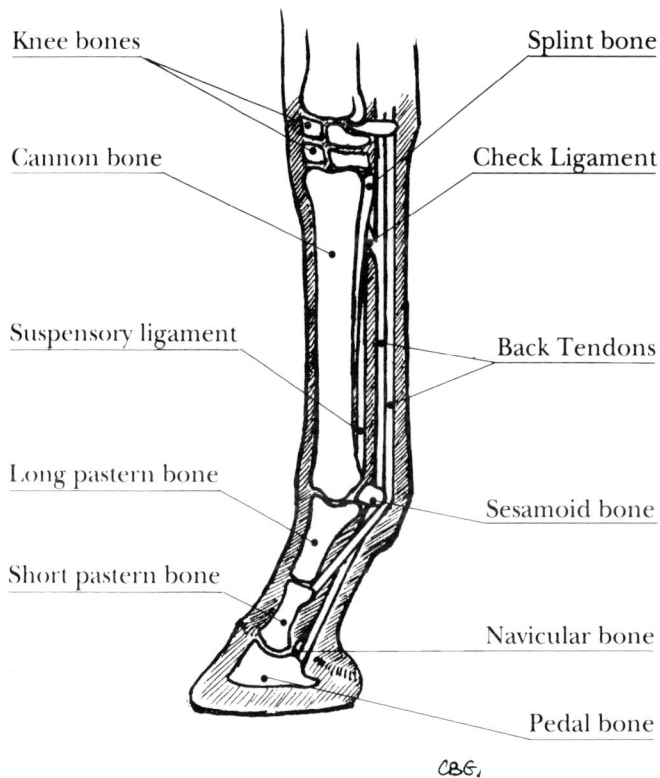

slightly. If a bad gash appears, it may need stitching and antibiotics, but for minor overreaches keep the wound clean and dry and treat with antibiotic powder or spray.

Curbs

These are sprained ligaments on the hind legs due to weak hocks and excessive strain on hard or sticky ground. A protusion appears below the point of the hock which causes lameness. The pony will have to be rested, until the ligaments are recovered.

Brushing

This occurs when the fetlock or coronet is struck by the

opposite foot. If the pony moves too close through a conformation fault, bad shoeing will make the problem worse. Make sure your farrier shapes the inside of the foot away from the middle.

Capped Hocks
A large swelling on the hock or elbow which is caused by contact with a hard surface. This is sometimes due to the pony lying on a hard surface if there is not sufficient bedding, or kicking the stable or horse box.

Spavin
There are two types of spavin, both found on the inside of the hock joint: bog spavin is a soft swelling and bone spavin is a bony enlargement. Sometimes the pony may be lame if he has a bone spavin. The movement of the hock is usually affected and the pony may drag his toe. The treatment is rest for perhaps several months with cold-water hosing.

Windgalls
Soft swellings around the fetlock joints found in young ponies who have been subject to work on hard ground and old ponies as a result of constant wear. The swellings usually go down and they cause no trouble. There is no treatment, but such swellings are a warning that the young ponies should be restricted from too much hard ground work, so they do not get worse.

Thoroughpins
Soft swellings just in front of the point of the hock which rarely cause lameness.

Navicular Disease
Caused by arthritic damage to the navicular bone which produces severe lameness. Sometimes the lameness improves with light work, but you should consult your vet who will prescribe treatment, and perhaps take X-rays to see how advanced the condition is.

Ponies with navicular are not sound, and only have a limited working life. Their shoes need checking by the farrier regularly, and they should not be ridden on hard ground. Navicular disease is accelerated by concussion on the hard ground.

Pedal Ostitis
Seldom occurs in ponies, but due to jarring to the pedal bone. Again, work on soft ground and special shoeing will help the pony.

Sesamoiditis
Produced by injury of the sesamoid bones situated behind the fetlock causing lameness.

Sidebones
Bony growths of the foot in the heel area due to hardening of the cartilages causing lameness through concussion and jarring.

Ringbones
Bony enlargements of the pastern bones caused by concussion and jarring. You will have to rest your pony.

Bruised Soles
This occurs when the sole of the foot is damaged and you can see redness when the feet are trimmed. It is usually caused by rough, hard ground and your farrier can advise how a pad can be shod on to the pony's foot.

Corns
These occur in the heel region of the foot, beneath the heels of the shoe. They generally happen in the fore feet due to bad shoeing. Your farrier will cut the corn out, and he must put on an adjusted shoe so that it does not put pressure on to the seat of the corn. Corns are painful and your pony may be lame.

Cracked Heels and Mud Fever
They are caused by bad stable management in not drying the heels properly in cold, wet weather. They are irritating and painful, and to cure you must keep the heels very dry. Vaseline or other grease can be used to prevent this condition in wet weather, but if it does not clear up you should obtain some ointment from your vet. Mud fever is caused by wet mud not being removed properly. White socks are prone to this, as the skin is not so tough. The skin becomes inflamed; scabs appear and flake off bringing the hair off with them. Again, obtain some ointment from your vet and keep the legs dry. In very wet weather and going, mud fever can arise on the body, particularly under the belly and around the girth. To prevent mud fever, dry the mud off, or if you wash a clipped pony you must dry it thoroughly with clean towels, or even a hair dryer.

Sandcrack
A splint in the outer wall of the hoof, going downwards from the coronet. Dry, brittle feet mainly cause this and hoof oil or conditioning foot treatment will help as a remedy. In bad cases you will have to ask your farrier to treat the foot with riveting, or special cutting away of the wall of the foot.

Seedy Toe
This condition causes damage, in the form of disintegration of the horn of the foot, to the toe between the outer and inner walls of the hoof. If your pony has this condition, which is rare, your farrier will draw your attention to it during shoeing and will advise you on the treatment.

Thrush
This is a common disease of the frog, and is caused by dirty stables affecting the pony's foot. It has a bad smell and is cured by the feet being picked out

regularly, scrubbing, drying the feet and treating with antibiotic spray.

If lameness does not clear up quickly you will have to consult your vet. As we have pointed out, ponies are naturally very sound. Lameness in ponies is not as common as it is for horses. We have given this guide so that you are aware of some of the types of lameness which may occur.

Lameness is a detailed and complex subject and if you are in any doubt you should call your vet. Very little lameness clears up of its own accord quickly; there is always a deep-seated reason for your pony being lame. The earlier you call the vet the quicker you are to getting your pony better; most conditions are best dealt with quickly before they get worse.

Some problems do not cause lameness and only matter if you wish to participate in top-class showing. The result of showing classes depends on competition between sound ponies, and any unsoundness or abnormality is marked accordingly. Some minor disorders do not matter at all at smaller shows, providing the pony is not lame.

Your Medicine Cupboard

You should begin to collect a small medicine cupboard which must be kept clean and away from your grooming kit and equipment. It is a good idea to store bandages in polythene bags to keep them clean, tidy and not affected by damp. You do not need a great collection, as you should not seek to avoid calling your vet. Here are some suggestions:
Animal lintex for treatment of wounds and sprains.
Antibiotic powder.
Antiseptic disinfectant.
Bandages.
Cotton wool.
Gamgee for cold water dressings and dry wounds.
Scissors and thermometer.

Ointment for cracked heels.

Equine Influenza

This is caused by an infectious and contagious virus. Ponies go off their food, lose weight and become weak. The nose and eyes may inflame and discharge. The pony's temperature will rise and he may cough.

You will have to keep him warm, dry and rested and isolated from others. You should call your vet to make sure he is not contracting pneumonia.

If there is an epidemic in your region, then avoid meeting other ponies if you have not vaccinated your pony.

Influenza Vaccination

This prevents equine influenza. Your vet will inject your pony twice within six weeks, then again in six months, and thereafter within every twelve months. It is important to keep a proper record of the dates of injections to ensure they are administered properly.

It is a sensible idea to vaccinate your pony if you wish to ride and compete regularly. Some pony clubs insist on ponies with vaccination certificates for camps, and some horse shows – mainly the larger ones – make it compulsory. This avoids spreading the virus. Sometimes, it only takes one pony with this virus at an event to spread it to many others.

Ponies should have light work only for three to four days after vaccination.

Tetanus

This is a serious disease resulting from a germ in the soil which gets into a wound. Humans can also contract tetanus in a similar way. Tetanus is also known as lockjaw, as the jaw literally becomes locked and the pony becomes stiff. A high temperature is a symptom. Tetanus can be fatal so early veterinary treatment is essential.

Tetanus Vaccination

It is advisable to give your pony a tetanus vaccination at the same time as the equine influenza. The tetanus part of the injection is inexpensive. If you decide against the equine influenza vaccination, you should definitely undertake the tetanus one. Fortunately, tetanus is now extremely rare, thanks to the majority of ponies being vaccinated nowadays.

Your Pony's Teeth

As a routine measure you can have your pony's teeth checked by the vet at the time of his annual vaccinations. Most of the time they will be in order, but occasionally older ponies need their teeth filed (called rasping) evenly. Sometimes they may have a festering or rotten tooth for removal, but you may see this swelling from outside the jaw. Wolf teeth are small teeth in front of the top molars which interfere with the action of the bit. They usually cause trouble in young ponies, and can easily be removed by your vet as they only have shallow roots.

Your Pony's Temperature

A pony's temperature is the same as that of a horse, 100.5°F (38°C). Any variation above 2° is not normal and you should call your vet.

Taking a Pony's Temperature

You should not attempt this until you are shown the procedure by an experienced person and you have some practice in reading thermometers.

A pony's temperature is not taken from his mouth as in humans. He does not understand not to bite the thermometer. It is taken under the tail in the rectum. Shake the thermometer down until the mercury level is below 100°F. Insert the bulb end into the rectum, until half the thermometer is inserted. Leave it in place for one minute and hold firmly. Take the thermometer out and read the scale. Wash it in water and disinfectant.

Your Pony's Pulse

The normal pulse rate is between 36 and 45 beats per minute. This is quite difficult to read until you have had some practice and the best place to feel your pony's pulse is under the top of the lower jaw.

Bandaging

Bandages are used for veterinary reasons as well as for travelling. You can also bandage your pony's legs to keep them warm and dry if he has been out in the cold.

Try to practise bandaging, so that you become used to it before it is urgently necessary. You should always bandage both front and back legs or all four legs. If a pony hurts one leg, he automatically puts more weight and strain on the opposite leg, so it has to be given more support.

Stable bandages are thick, slightly elasticated and about four inches wide. Make sure the tapes, or Velcro fastenings, are rolled to the inside.

Animal Lintex or gamgee padding should be placed under the bandage. The bandage should be

Putting on stable or travelling bandages: crouch down to perform this task. Do not kneel as you will not be able to move away if your pony does not stand still. Start by wrapping the bandage round the leg in a clockwise direction, using the end with the tapes, just below the knee.

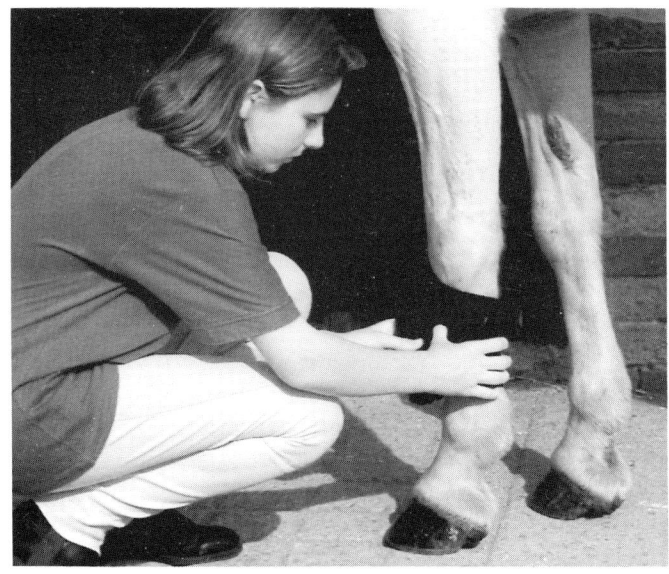

FIT FOR ANYTHING

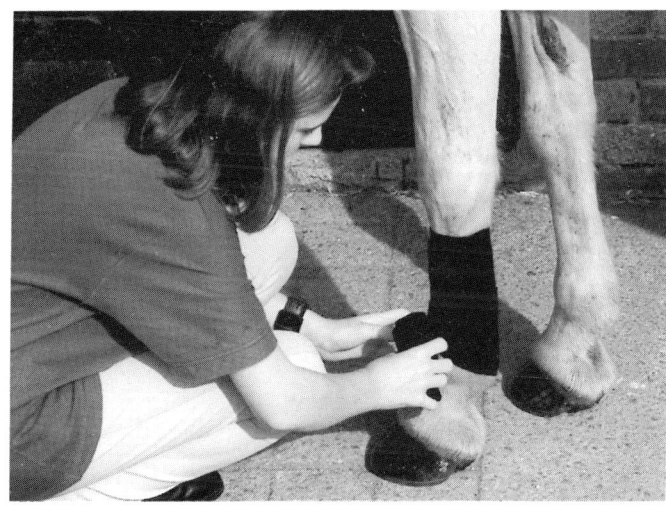

Work downwards toward the fetlock, covering the joint, then continue bandaging upwards. Tie the tapes in the middle of the cannon bone on the outside.

wound from just under the knee, or hock, to just below the fetlock joint.

Hold the bandage at a slight angle to the leg and leave a loose end about three quarters of an inch long. Make your first turn, then fold the loose end down, and wrap the bandage over it with the second turn. This helps to keep the bandage secure so that it does not slip. You will have to keep it fairly tight at this stage, so that you can get a grip. This is the most important stage of the bandaging and if this is not correct, then the bandage will not hold. Overlap each turn by a half of the bandage's width, and try to mould the bandage to the shape of the leg. Do not turn it too tightly at this stage. It is not necessary and may damage the tendons. Try to finish where you started bandaging, and tie the tapes or Velcro at the outside of the leg. Tying with a knot at the back of the leg may damage the tendons if the bandage is left on too long. Tie the tapes in a neat bow and tuck the ends firmly into the tape already wound round the leg.

When you take off the bandage undo the fastenings and pass the slack bandage from hand to hand quickly before your pony treads over it.

9 *In the Saddle*

You will probably want to own a pony because you love riding. Your pony will be a working partner as well as a friend.

Hacking across countryside is wonderful and so is your involvement with a pony. A good partnership between your pony and yourself is to be gained by riding.

Riding experience cannot be acquired quickly. It takes years to learn, but it is enjoyable at every level. Even grown-ups who have spent a lifetime learning to ride are still learning.

Most children start to ride at about nine or ten. Of course, there are good riders younger than this, but very young children often do not have sufficient balance or coordination, and may become frightened. Small children's feet can get trodden on and riding in the wet and cold in the winter can spoil their enjoyment perhaps for ever.

An indoor school is a good place in which to learn to ride. My daughter started riding in an indoor school, and we found she gained confidence this way. Ponies are easily controllable in a school and are quite used to going around it. They are not easily distracted in a school, and young children find them easy to stop there.

If you have horsey parents, or an older brother or sister riding, then you will probably be taught to ride at home. Other children usually start at a riding school.

IN THE SADDLE

Standards vary at different establishments. Have a look round those in your area before deciding which one to attend. Riding schools have to be licensed by law. At a good riding school there should be a qualified instructor with a BHSAI certificate (British Horse Society's Assistant Instructor). This is a qualification which involves much training, the higher qualification is BHSI (British Horse Society Instructor).

Your riding school may have facilities where you can learn stable management. This will help you if you are hoping to have your own pony. Looking after ponies should be almost as much fun as riding.

We shall first explain riding for beginners and later more advanced riding.

Mounting

There is a correct way to get on to your pony. You should learn the right way; it will become easier with practice. You will be helped first of all, but the aim is

Mounting your pony: facing your pony's tail, collect up the reins and whip in your left hand. Put your left foot into the stirrup, avoiding kicking the pony with your toe. Grasp the cantle of the saddle in your right hand.

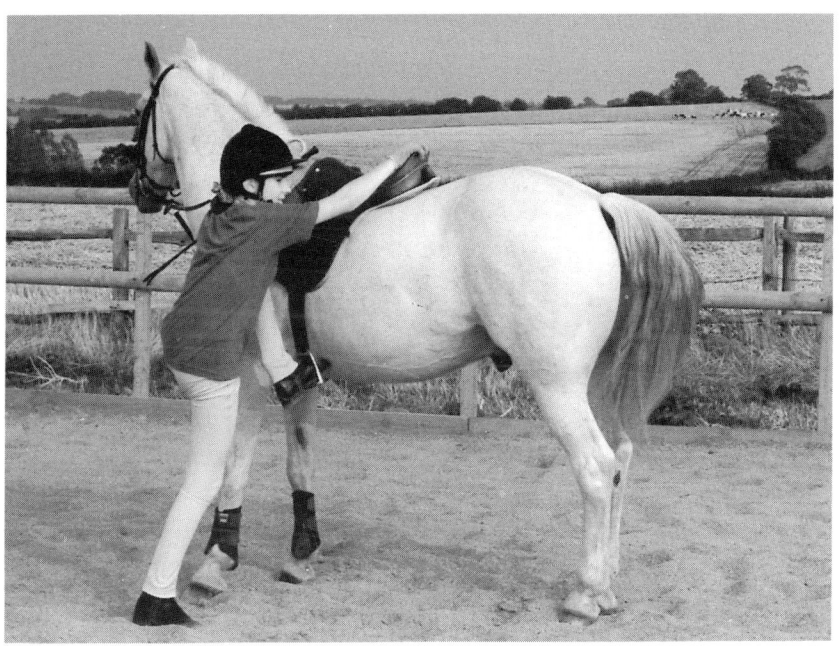

YOUR PONY

Swing up into the saddle keeping your right leg and foot clear of the cantle and your pony's back. Try to mount lightly with the minimum of fuss. Do not plonk heavily into the saddle.

to be able to get on to your pony keeping him under control.

First check the length of your stirrups by putting your left wrist up to the stirrup bar. The bottom of the stirrup should reach down to your armpit. It helps to have the stirrups your approximate length before you try to mount.

Stand on the nearside with your back to his head. Hold both reins in your left hand and throw the loop from the reins over to the offside, so that you do not get your foot tangled in it. You can also hold part of the mane in the reins to give you more support and avoid hurting your pony's mouth.

Take hold of the stirrup iron in your right hand, and pull it towards you, so that you can put your left foot in it firmly. Spring up and hold the back of the saddle with your right hand to steady yourself, and then swing your right leg over the saddle. Try to

IN THE SADDLE

avoid poking your toe into the pony's side, and lower yourself gently into the saddle so that your pony is not alarmed.

You should then check the length of your stirrups. Take your feet out of the stirrups. The bottom of the iron should be in line with the ankle bone. Do not forget to check your girth. Put the reins in one hand, lift your leg forward and upwards. Reach down and pull the girth straps one at a time to alter them. Do not tighten them both together as you may miss the girth holes and you will suddenly find your saddle slipping.

Dismounting: take BOTH feet from the stirrups, swing your right leg over the cantle, retaining the reins and stick in your left hand which takes your weight on the withers. For safety, do not dismount any other way.

Dismounting

Take both feet out of the stirrup irons. It is dangerous to leave your left foot in. Gather both reins into your left hand and keep a feel on the reins to prevent your pony moving. Hold the pommel of the saddle with your right hand and swing your right leg over the back of the saddle.

Try and remember to bend your knees as you land to stop hurting your feet.

Your Position in the Saddle

The position in the saddle is known as the seat. Your aim is to have a seat in the saddle that is not dependent on the reins or the stirrups. When you begin riding you will need security from the reins and stirrups, but as you become experienced you will become firmer in the saddle.

You should sit in the saddle as if a straight line is drawn connecting your shoulder, hip joint and heel. Your hands are to indicate to your pony through the reins. You should not rely on them to hold on, although this is easier said than done at first.

A useful rhyme to remember is:

> Your head and your heart keep up,
> Your hands and your heels keep down,
> Your knees keep into your pony's sides,
> And your elbows into your own.

Ponies are taught to respond to different aids, or signals, when they are broken-in and trained.

Natural Aids

These are the rider's weight, legs, hands and voice.

Weight

A well-trained and schooled pony will respond to the various shiftings and balance of his rider's body. This means he anticipates a change in direction or speed.

Legs
The legs are used together with the seat to drive a pony forwards from his hindquarters. A well-schooled pony should not need touching with your heels; a squeeze from the calves is generally sufficient.

Hands
The rider keeps contact with the pony's forehand through the reins. You should always keep a light contact with your pony's mouth even when relaxing.

Voice
Ponies will listen to your voice. Use it to tell your pony what to do if he is slow to respond to your other aids. Say, for example, 'Whoa' or 'Trot on'. To calm him down and give him confidence if he is frightened use 'Steady on' or 'Walk on past'.

Artificial Aids
These are sticks, whips, spurs and martingales. You use these to help the natural aids, but they are not substitutes.

Walking
To make your pony move off at a walk, make sure your reins are short, squeeze his sides and urge him forward by pushing downwards and forwards through the saddle. If he does not respond you will have to kick him gently behind the girth with your heels.

Try not to move forwards in the saddle, and keep looking ahead through the pony's ears.

Turning
To turn to the left, gently pull the left rein and squeeze with both legs, the left leg at the girth and the right leg slightly further back.

To turn to the right reverse the procedure. Once the pony has turned then relax the aids.

Halting
You will probably want to halt fairly early. This will give you confidence to know you can stop if you wish. Squeeze your legs against your pony's sides and then feel the mouth so that you can tell your pony you wish to stop and at the same time brace your body so you do not go forward.

As soon as you have halted loosen the reins slightly or your pony may try to go backwards.

The Trot
When you can walk confidently, you will begin to trot. Trotting is quite a difficult pace to learn. It is a knack of rising and sitting in time to your pony's steps. You will probably bounce about to begin with, and then suddenly realize how to do it.

The aids to trot are the same as those to walk. Shorten the reins, and use your legs by squeezing or kicking gently if needed. Hold on to the neck strap if you feel insecure, but practice will make you more secure in the saddle. Keep your heels down. You will soon get the rhythm if you count one, two, one, two, to yourself. Practise standing in the stirrups, then sitting when the pony is standing still before you urge him to walk and then trot.

It is easier to rise to the trot than to sit, but more advanced riding involves learning how to sit to the trot as well.

The Canter
It is easier to sit to the canter than the trot but this is a faster pace. The aids are the same as for walking and trotting. If your pony just trots faster, then you should feel his mouth more and squeeze or kick more firmly. When he canters and you feel in control, slacken your reins a little. Cantering should be comfortable and exciting.

The Gallop

Galloping is a faster version of cantering. You should not try this pace until you have been riding some time. You will find it best to let this happen naturally, perhaps when out hacking with friends. You will suddenly realize your pony is going much faster than a canter.

Ponies tend to get excited galloping along with others. It is natural for them to do this on their native moorland, and you may find your pony will always want to go faster and overtake the others. If you are worried that you cannot stop your pony properly, you should try to avoid galloping until you are in complete control.

More Advanced Riding

So far we have only explained the beginning stages of riding. To ride properly and to jump you need to understand more about the basic paces of your pony. Riding needs to be learned slowly and practised often.

To school your pony you need an area long enough to circle him easily. Ideally this should be flat, and either fenced, or, at least hedged along two sides. You can use open spaces, but it is usually more difficult to get your pony to concentrate unless there is at least partial enclosure.

Ponies can get bored and naughty being schooled in their own fields, so you may have to look elsewhere to find a suitable place. You may know of someone locally with a sand school or schooling area you can use. Some of the best places are the quiet corners of a field or bridleway found out hacking. It does not have to be expensive or even marked out. We know the best areas on our exercise rides. One is in the corner of a field with a gated ride and the other a grass area by a quiet cross roads of lanes.

They are both a ten minute hack from the field or stable – just enough time to warm up going there and cool off coming back.

YOUR PONY

Walking

Once you are secure in the saddle you must make your pony stride out well. It is all too easy just to let him amble along following the pony in front, but this is not good enough.

Walking is a four beat pace: you achieve a good walk by keeping an elastic but constant feel of the pony's mouth through the reins, and urge him forward with your body and legs. If he is sluggish you will have to kick him on, but you should be squeezing him forward all the time, and moving with him, not just sitting on top of him. You will begin to feel his stride lengthening and you will come on to the bit, so that his neck arches better.

Ride your pony in large circles in a schooling area, and change the rein so your pony becomes practised at listening to you. You can work a pony better in a circle; keep him turning, changing the rein, or moving in figures of eight.

Occasionally practise a good halt, and then move

When schooling your pony practise coming to a balanced, collected halt at a marker. The rider still maintains an even contact with the mouth.

IN THE SADDLE

on. Schooling your pony like this will make him concentrate and listen to you. He cannot know what you are about to ask him to do, and will become attentive and alert. Young riders sometimes make the mistake of going aimlessly round in circles which is not only boring for them, but also for their ponies.

Trotting

To ride correctly at the trot you have to understand what your pony's legs are doing. The pony springs into the air and lands on the ground on each pair of diagonals in turn. The trot is a two beat pace.

There are two pairs of diagonals. You are on the left diagonal when your seat returns to the saddle when the near fore and the off hind legs come to the ground, and the right diagonal with the off fore and near hind legs. You change diagonals when you change direction by sitting down in the saddle for an extra beat.

You should aim to sit on the left diagonal when on

At the trot keep your pony between your hands and your heels, using enough impulsion to produce a nice, extended stride. This pony is going nicely, but the reins are slightly too slack and the weight of the rider is marginally forward resulting in the rider's heel being up and her toe down.

the right rein to be correct and vice versa. Try and practise this. If you are interested in showing and dressage, then it will be especially important to get it right.

The Extended Trot

A well-schooled pony will be able to carry out an extended trot if required. This is also part of dressage. The extended trot is where the stride is increased, not just the speed. When you are trotting, you squeeze strongly with your legs, feel the mouth and push with your seat. Your pony's stride should lengthen, his neck will stretch out, and his action become more flowing and comfortable. Your pony may try and canter but the difference of the aids between extended trot and canter is the balance between hand and leg pressure.

Cantering

The canter is a three-beat pace. During the canter one foreleg is always in front of the other. A well-schooled pony will always move off and lead with the inside leg when cantering in a circle. This is called being 'on the correct leg'.

If you are cantering along in a straight line you will not have to worry which leg you are on, but it is important to get your pony on the correct (inside) leg for circle work. You will need to do this for all aspects of riding. Even if you never intend to compete, you will find it very unbalanced and uncomfortable to be on the wrong leg at a canter.

To get on the correct leg at a canter, for example, the off fore when you are trotting on the right rein: stop rising, and sit at the trot. Feel the right rein, and squeeze with both legs, the left leg further back behind the girth. Reverse the aids on the other rein.

You should not bend down to see which leg your pony is on. Practise feeling if he is on the correct leg. You may find your pony prefers to lead on one leg

IN THE SADDLE

more than the other. Most ponies do so. Find out which this is, and when you want him on the other 'worst' leg you must give him more definite aids.

It is best to ask your pony to strike off at a canter on a corner, so he will be balanced to get on the right leg. If you are worried that he may pull or buck, then ask him to canter alongside the fence or hedge, to keep more control.

Counter Canter

This is more advanced riding: the pony is deliberately

At the canter sit 'into' your pony, keeping a responsive contact with the pony's mouth on the reins. This pony is going well on the inside rein.

made to canter with the outside leg leading, with his head and body turned on the opposite rein. You may not have attained the stage of dressage for this, but you should have an idea of what is involved.

Disunited Canter
When a pony canters normally, he has one pair of laterals (the two legs on one side of his body) in front of the opposite pair. With a disunited canter, one pair of diagonals is placed in front of the other. This is most uncomfortable, and you should bring the pony back to a trot and start again.

Galloping
You must have full control of your pony to gallop him effectively. You must always choose suitable ground or 'going' as it is known. This is sensible because galloping can cause damage to your mount's legs.

Hard ground causes jarring and strain on the bones, tendons and ligaments. The forelegs are especially prone to damage as most of the weight of the horse and the rider comes down through the forelegs to the ground. Heavy going and uneven ground can also cause strain.

Try to choose ground with plenty of 'give'. It should be soft enough to see an imprint of your pony's hoof. You should always maintain contact with the pony's mouth for control, and this will also mean that he is more balanced, lessening the strain on his legs.

If you gallop out hacking and your pony gets too excited, just think what might happen if he got loose. He may try to gallop more, so gallop well away from open roads. If you should fall off then your pony will not run into harm. Busy roads can so easily cause accidents to ponies, particularly with today's heavy traffic levels.

If you are galloping for a length of time, perhaps

when hunter trialling or hunting, raise yourself out of the saddle, taking your weight on your knees and your heels. This eases your pony's back, and it is the most comfortable position for you. It also helps you to keep contact with the pony's mouth. However, you may tire until you are fit. Race riders are extremely fit. Experienced hunting people spend much of the day keeping as much weight as possible out of the saddle.

Think ahead when you are galloping. Everything happens much faster. Try to give your pony plenty of time to decrease speed. If you halt quickly you will put strain on your pony's legs and you may skid badly.

Rein Back

This means to go backwards. Ponies will move backwards only for a few strides. Squeeze your pony's sides strongly with your legs just behind the girth, and keep a firm feel on the reins but do not pull them. If your pony moves forwards, keep restraining him with the reins and continue to use your legs.

If your pony does not understand what to do, as he has not been properly trained or has not been recently schooled, ask a friend to help by standing by his head and pushing him backwards while you try again. Many ponies understand better if you use your voice telling them to back.

After moving backwards a few strides, as straight as possible, you should move forwards again. This is because the pony may get confused by the aids to halt and moving back. This could encourage him to rein back when you want to halt.

Going 'On the Bit'

A well-balanced, schooled pony naturally holds his head so that his weight is balanced evenly between the forehand and the hind quarters. By accepting the bit your pony accepts the contact of your hands on the reins and his body becomes balanced.

Your pony should not resist contact with his mouth and will respond willingly to the hand aids. When a pony is on the bit his head is held in a proud, graceful manner, and he will be alert for your next aids.

A good head carriage cannot be maintained unless you have 'good hands'. Many riders are too heavy handed, or their ponies are over-bitted. 'Good hands' means a light and skilful contact with the reins, understanding the mouth of your pony. Too many ponies' mouths are ruined permanently by riders with heavy hands. This often occurs because riders are using too much contact with their hands, and not enough pressure with their legs, and seat.

Your Seat

You should aim to achieve a strong independent seat so that you do not rely on the reins to hang on. This can only be achieved with practice and experience, but you should try to understand what you are aiming for. It is good to ride a well-balanced and schooled pony so that you know how it feels when a pony is going well. A pony should be on the bit at all paces, so that he will be a comfortable, balanced and responsive ride. Very well-schooled ponies are said to be able to be ridden 'on the little finger'.

You should allow the pony to stretch his neck and head by releasing the reins for a few minutes when relaxing.

Riding without stirrups will help you develop a stronger seat, and you should try to practise this whenever you can, but do not attempt it if you feel very unsafe. It is easy to lose control.

Young riders are especially supple and that is why it is best to start riding while still young.

When attempting to ride without stirrups, start at

the walk, and certainly do not canter until you feel confident. It does feel insecure at first. You must cross your stirrups over in front of the saddle to save your ankles from getting bruised; try to keep your heels down.

Only try bareback riding when you are more experienced. It is difficult, slippery and easy to fall off. Those of us who rode ponies bareback when we were children found it a great help in developing a safe seat.

There are several exercises you can practise which will help you become firmer in the saddle, and develop your muscles for riding. At first your pony should be held by a parent or instructor. It is important that your pony does not move or it will be dangerous for you.

Your helper should stand in front of the pony, and hold a rein in each hand either side of the bit. My daughter had a nasty fall on a pony because it suddenly became alarmed and galloped off.

Release the reins and put your stick down. Try to remember the ideal seat when you carry out the exercises. If you can carry them out easily, move on to the more difficult ones. Keep practising them until you find them all easy. They are good fun.

Exercise 1
Stretch both arms straight above you in the air. Bring your hands down to your hips. Stand up in your stirrups with your hands still on your hips. Sit down slowly, and do not thump into the saddle.

Exercise 2
Fold your arms. Lean slowly backwards until your head touches the pony's croup. Come back again to the upright position, and go forwards until you face the mane.

Exercise 3
Touch your toes on each foot with the opposite hand three or four times.

Exercise 4
Hold out both arms straight at shoulder level. Swing them from left to right, moving the top half of your body.

Excercise 5
'Round the World'. This is a favourite with young riders. Take your feet out of the stirrups, and swing your left leg over your pony's neck to sit sideways on the saddle. Then swing your right leg over the croup so that you are facing his tail. Bring your left leg over the croup, and then your right leg back over the neck so that you are back where you started. Then go the other way round.

You can perform these exercises while moving at a walk or a trot, but it is always sensible to have someone leading you. Do not try them until your pony is quiet, standing still and you can do the exercises easily.

Lungeing
Lungeing is circling your pony around you from the ground, using a lungeing rein about twenty feet long. This is a way of schooling and exercising your pony without tiring yourself.

The pony can either be ridden or schooled unmounted. Lungeing is a good way of learning to ride, and your initial riding should include some lungeing. You will not have to think about controlling the pony while he is on the lunge, and so you can concentrate on becoming balanced and improving your seat in the saddle.

For lungeing, your pony will need to wear a lungeing cavesson. This is a head collar with a strong

IN THE SADDLE

It is preferable to use a lungeing cavesson for ground work, fitted securely, we suggest, over a bridle so that your pony's head can be held by the bridle reins if necessary. Attach the lunge line to the middle front ring on the cavesson noseband. Ensure the bridle reins are held in place behind the stirrups which should be put up. Stand in line with the pony's quarters and drive on with the end of the lunge line. Do not use a whip. Try to maintain an even, balanced pace at walk, trot and canter and lunge in both directions.

noseband, having metal rings on the front. You can buy canvas pony varieties which are cheaper than leather. Fit the cavesson over the bridle quite tightly so that it cannot slip, and be careful to avoid the cheekstraps slipping over the eye. The noseband should fit just above the bit, slightly lower than a normal noseband.

The lungeing rein is made of webbing, so that it does not get ruined by dragging on the ground. The end of the rein will have a swivel to attach on to the middle ring of the noseband. At the other end of the rein is a loop. It is a bad practice to hold this loop as you can get your hand caught in it and you may be dragged. Instead hold the rein about two or three yards from the end, leaving some slack for your right hand.

If the pony is saddled, run the stirrups up and put the reins behind the stirrups.

You should practise riding on the lunge, and lunge your pony from the centre of the circle. If your pony is used to going on the lunge it is quite easy. To move him off, walk behind his quarters, and use your voice to encourage him to walk on. You must be careful at this stage that you do not get kicked. Watch your pony's hind quarters all the time. If he bucks he could reach and hurt you. Once he is out of range you can concentrate on the way he circles. Stand level with his quarters so that you can drive him on. We find it best not to use a lunge whip. The majority of ponies will lunge well if you use the spare end of the lunge rein to twirl about and drive them on.

Use your voice and talk to him, telling him to walk on, trot on and whoa. You must be definite about what you want your pony to do on the lunge. If you are not, you may find your pony stops and just looks in at you.

Some ponies have not been taught to walk on the lunge, and move off immediately into a spanking trot. You will have to steady this type. It is not ideal to let them whizz round and round.

To stop your pony, gently feel the lunge rein to restrain him and voice 'Whoa'. You may have to do this a few times before he slows down and stops. If you cannot stop your pony then make the circle smaller by drawing him in and saying 'Whoa'. You may have to use the lunge rein strongly.

Trotting on the lunge is quite sufficient until you are experienced and can control your pony cantering. Cantering needs to be controlled or it tends to be too fast and your pony can stumble or slip.

Lungeing is useful to get some of the energy out of a pony before riding. If he has a good trot or canter on the lunge he is usually not quite so exuberant when you ride. Be sure to avoid his heels if he bucks.

If your pony suffers from laminitis, lungeing is a good way to give a good deal of exercise in a limited time. Even parents who do not ride can get the knack of lungeing.

Some experienced horsemen lunge with two reins, the other rein coming around the further side of the pony and behind his hocks. We think this is quite difficult for young riders so one lunge rein is sufficient. If you do try it, hold the further rein up so your pony cannot tread on it.

Long Reining

The aim of long reining is to drive your pony on from behind and get him used to steering and turning. Most young ponies are long reined during their training, but it is a good way of building up their neck and quarter muscles at any time.

In long reining the pony is driven from behind by two lunge reins along his sides up to the two rings on the side of the cavesson noseband.

You will need an assistant for this. Experienced horsemen can long rein on their own, but it takes a

YOUR PONY

good deal of skill and strength to control a horse or pony long reining.

Put on the cavesson with two lunge reins and thread the reins through the stirrups, making sure they can travel through the stirrups without knotting.

Take the reins back one at a time about ten feet behind the pony, and lay them on the ground. Be careful not to touch the pony's sides with the reins. Some ponies do not like this, and if you have trouble you should spend longer getting the pony used to long reins around his back legs.

Next pick up the reins from behind the pony, and walk forward, using your voice to drive the pony on. Your assistant should walk round with the pony, maintaining light contact with a lead rein.

When you are long reining, make your pony walk forward and stride out. Practise turning by feeling

Long reining: hold your pony by the reins while the long reins are being sorted out. One person should lead the pony using the reins while the other uses the long reins attached to the cavesson to drive the pony forward. This avoids the risk of damage to the pony's mouth and the person leading the pony can prevent it taking off.

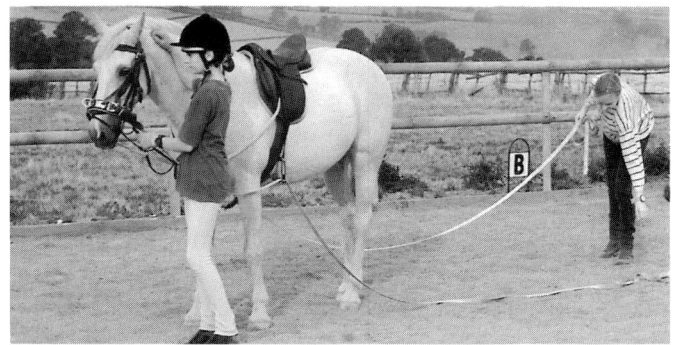

the left, and right reins, and if you want the pony to walk on more, use your voice and slap the outside rein against his leg just above the hock.

To halt, equally restrain both lunge reins and tell him to 'Whoa'.

Long reining is only carried out at a walk. You would find it too exhausting to trot.

When long reining and lungeing you should make much of your pony, and let him know you are pleased with him. Without your leg aids he has to listen to you far more. Both lungeing and long reining are quite concentrated work for your pony.

If you get in a muddle with the reins and your pony gets his legs over them, stop, and put the reins on the ground. Your assistant should hold him quietly, so that you can come forward to unravel. Be careful your pony is not alarmed and be aware that he may strike out if he has the reins tightly around his heels.

Pony Club Rallies

Attending Pony Club rallies will give you the opportunity of instruction to improve your riding and jumping.

You will be placed in a group of young riders all of similar experience. Riding instruction and schooling takes place first, followed by show jumping or cross country.

Pony Club Camp

Pony Club camp takes place in the summer holidays. Camps are divided into ages: the younger members travel to camp every day while the older members stay in caravans or tents. Camp usually lasts a week and is the ideal opportunity for you to learn all aspects of caring for your pony, riding and jumping. Every part of the day is supervised and there are many competitions organized. The week is good fun, especially spent with other young riders.

10 *Road Sense*

We aim to help you enjoy your riding, but things can go wrong. Riding is a risk sport. Ignorance is not bliss in horsemanship; you can take sensible precautions to lessen the risk.

One place where the risks are increasing is on our busy roads. Nowadays, all too many vehicle drivers know nothing about horses and ponies. They are inclined to drive past them too fast and too close. If a nervous or excitable pony steps out suddenly into the path of a car or lorry the result can be a very nasty accident.

As a rider there is much that you can do to lessen the risks when you take your pony on the roads.

We have already stressed the importance of riding a pony which is not frightened of road traffic. A pony which has had a bad experience on the roads, and shies or bolts from traffic, is very dangerous and must not be taken on the roads until its behaviour has improved, which is unlikely unless it is trained by a very experienced, older rider.

But, assuming your pony is traffic proof, there is still a lot that you can do to make riding on the roads safer.

Whenever possible use bridle paths or use roads which have ridable grass verges which enable you to keep off the road surface.

Here are some of the basic rules which you must remember to carry out when you have to ride on the roads.

Always ride on the left. If you are with other ponies, try to keep in single file on very narrow roads or lanes, and especially on bends.

It is possible to guard against your pony swinging out into the path of traffic. Do not slop along, riding on a loose rein. Keep proper contact with your pony's mouth and be ready to use your legs instantly. Sometimes, even a quiet pony will shy out into the road because it has seen something startling at the side of the road on its left, for example, a barking dog rushing to a gateway as you pass by.

If you feel your pony about to shy, exert pressure with your right leg, which is the leg on the outside as you ride along on the left. At the same time shorten your right rein; this will swing his head to the right, and will stop him swinging his hindquarters out suddenly in front of vehicles.

Practise this when no problem arises, and you will find it all the easier to do if trouble occurs.

Try to anticipate trouble before it arises. If a lorry approaches with a flapping tarpaulin over the load it can alarm any pony or horse. Sometimes tractors with lift forks on the front can frighten ponies and horses. Use your legs to push your pony forward, shorten your reins, make sure you have your pony well controlled 'between hand and heel', and keep him moving forward, well into the left-hand side of the road.

If you are riding with friends, make sure that the less experienced, or more excitable pony is kept on the inside if the road is wide enough to allow you to ride in pairs.

If you are turning right, look round over your

shoulder to check whether traffic is coming before you move over. Put your right arm out clearly to indicate that you are going right. Similarly, put out your left arm when you are going left.

If you are worried that your pony is likely to misbehave when traffic overtakes you, put out your right hand and firmly wave it up and down to indicate to car and lorry drivers following you to slow down.

When a driver slows or halts for you, always thank him. Even a nod and a smile is better than nothing if you do not think he can hear you. Drivers do not like it when riders go past with their noses in the air when a driver has taken the trouble to interrupt his journey by slowing down. Good manners are especially important when you are up there on your pony. The same is true, by the way, if anyone on foot should open or close a farm gate for you. Always thank them properly. This is especially important when you are out hunting.

One big danger on the road for horses and ponies is the risk of slipping up on slippery patches. Modern roads, especially country lanes, become very smooth and slippery. Trotting or even walking on these slippery patches is like asking your pony to make his way across an ice rink. It is all too easy for him to slip and give you a nasty fall on the road's hard surface.

Usually, the inside edge of a road or lane closest to the kerb or hedgerow is rougher; keep on this as much as possible. If you live in a district where the roads are especially slippery, get your farrier to put special road studs in your pony's shoes. These help tremendously in avoiding slip-ups.

We hope you will usually be able to ride on the roads in the company of others, as herd animals like ponies and horses get a lot of comfort from travelling in groups rather than singly. But if you are riding on your own take special care: it is even more important that your pony is traffic proof. If you do have to ride on your own, make sure you tell someone your route.

We trust that you will not ride anywhere at all without putting on your safety skull cap, but it cannot be stressed too much, that it is especially important on the roads where any fall is on a hard surface.

Nowadays, many riders use special reflective clothing over their riding clothes to ensure that they are easily seen by vehicle drivers when there is poor light. This is a good idea, and well worth taking up. An alternative is reflective leg bands for your pony. You can find such items on the British Horse Society/Pony Club stand which attends major horse shows and horse trials, or you can send away for these things which are advertised in *Horse and Hound*.

We hope you will not attempt to ride your pony on the roads in darkness, but anyone attempting to do so should use stirrup lights which shine white to the front, and red to the rear, as well as reflective clothing.

One of the many advantages of joining the Pony Club is the opportunity to take their special test for riding safely on the road. It may seem a bit of a bore, but unfortunately, Britain's roads are so full of traffic, that the pony and the horse are in increasing danger every time they venture on to the public highway.

Your parents should make sure that your pony is insured, at least for third party risks. This means that if your pony causes damage to anyone else, or their property, at any time, you are insured if they make a claim against you. Obviously, the risks of this happening are at their greatest when on the roads, but it can occur at any time, especially if your pony should escape from his field or stable.

11 *Up and Away*

Jumping is exciting and thrilling. Most young riders are always yearning to jump their ponies.

When you can control your pony at a walk, trot and canter you will be sufficently balanced and steady in the seat to try jumping. As an introduction to jumping, first walk and then trot your pony over a pole on the ground. It should be a heavy pole so your pony can see it properly.

When you can trot over it, move into a canter over it, and you may find your pony will give a little jump.

Then raise the pole on some bricks so that it is about six inches off the ground and repeat. You should always have an instructor or parent with you when you start jumping.

Many people like to jump cavallettis which are poles fixed to cross-pieces at each end. The height varies from six to eighteen inches (15–45cm) depending on which part of the cross-piece is on the ground.

Alternatively, you can make your own jumps with poles and wooden blocks or bricks, so that you can vary the height easily. You can construct a line of little fences at intervals of about four feet (1.2m) depending on your pony's stride, and trot up and down these. You may have to shorten the length for a small pony. The object of the cavelletti is to train a young pony to look at what he is jumping, round his back and pick up his feet. They are used to train the young rider to develop a jumping seat.

UP AND AWAY

Site the cavellettis so that your pony will perform in a sensible mood. It is no use placing them downhill with a wide open space at the end or he is likely to become over excited!

Once you can trot over them try to canter. One or two cavellettis at a time is enough to start with, then increase up to three or four. Small fences or cavellettis should be about three yards (3m) apart.

If your pony rushes, go back to trotting. Ponies must not be allowed to rush. They are much harder to control. You must never feel your pony is going faster than you wish.

When you can jump this height, start to make the fence wider instead of higher. This will help you to learn the jumping style.

You should always try to have your pony 'on the bit', doing his flat work nicely between your hands and your legs. You should not try and jump until your pony is going like this. An important part of jumping is in the approach.

As you trot towards the jump, you should bring

When schooling your pony over jumps, start with a lower height. To make your pony look at the fence and concentrate trot him over a pole on the ground placed about ten feet in front of the fence, or less for a pony much smaller than 14 hh.

your weight slightly forward, but still maintain a contact with his mouth. Your legs should be closed firmly against his sides.

When your pony takes off he will push himself forward from his hindquarters. You must be prepared to swing your body forward to go with him. If you happen to get 'left behind' you will throw yourself and your pony off balance and jerk him in the mouth.

While you are in the air you must keep still, so that you do not distract your pony.

On landing, your pony will take his weight on his forelegs. You must swing back slightly to brace yourself against the pony's legs striking the ground. He will actually land on one foreleg a fraction of a second before the other.

Keep upright as your pony lands, and ride away from the jump. As he lands, keep contact with his mouth and release the reins to give him as much rein as he requires. Do not slacken the reins completely. You must keep a slight hold in case he stumbles, or tries to rush off afterwards.

At first you will find that you cannot think of everything at once and you will be over the fence in a flash. Somewhat surprisingly, as the fences get bigger it will all become easier; it is possible then to react more effectively to each stage of jumping. Do try to start jumping on an experienced, calm pony. You will soon gain confidence.

Finally reward your pony when he jumps well. Ponies like a pat down the neck, and it gives them encouragement. A small handful of grass when you finish jumping is always appreciated.

Remember: the most important rule of jumping is 'throw your heart over first!'

Lengths of Stirrups

When you start jumping higher fences you will find you need to shorten your stirrups a couple of holes.

To understand this, take your feet out of the stirrups, and fold yourself forwards from your hips. You will find it hard to balance, as your leg will slide backwards, and you will feel yourself leaning on your hands.

You do not need to shorten your stirrups more than a couple of holes or you will be jumping too short, and it will be easy for you to overbalance and go over your pony's head. You should not attempt to look like a jockey. You will need to practise to find the ideal length at which you feel comfortable.

Higher Fences

When you can jump small fences well, try a variety of jumps. There are endless ways to make up jumps with oil drums, hurdles, feed troughs, tyres, logs and numerous poles.

Always check fences to see they are safe to jump. You should not jump where the ground is badly rutted, and where there are rabbit holes or dangerous objects to land on. Do not attempt to build jumps next to or near barbed wire unless you can trust your pony. There have been bad accidents when ponies have tried to run out and jump the wire.

Many ponies do not like ditches so try to find several to jump while you are out on your hacks. If your pony is wary, follow another pony over. Start with tiny ditches first of all so that your pony just hops over. Some ponies take a big leap, and it is all too easy to catch them in the mouth. This will put them off jumping in the future.

If you have trouble with your pony, never be tempted to dismount to lead him over. You will pull him over, and he can easily land on you. Ponies always try to avoid treading on anything, but if you are holding the reins, there is nowhere else for him to go.

You may have to go out of your way to find a ditch or water, but it will pay off. Many ponies stop at

these obstacles when hunter trialling. If your pony will tackle these without hesitation you will have an advantage.

Problems

Refusing

A refusal is when a pony stops at the take-off. This happens for many reasons and it is important to work out why your pony refuses, so that you can correct this fault. A naughty pony may have been given the perfect conditions for jumping the fence, but still stops. This will be difficult for you to correct, and you should ask expert advice.

Most refusals are the rider's fault. You may be

UP AND AWAY

overfacing your pony and yourself by asking him to jump a fence too big or wide. It may have a difficult approach and you may not be giving him enough encouragement.

The ground may be too hard; perhaps you have jarred his legs. You may have been jerking him in the mouth, which he remembers only too well.

Your pony may be bored if you have been jumping him too much. You may not have been urging him on enough at a fence which he does not like the appearance of.

One of the most frequent cases for refusing is a pony being allowed to decrease his speed coming into the fence. You should always come into a fence calmly and steadily, and then urge your pony

Over upright fences it is more inviting for your pony to have a ground line i.e. a pole on the ground under the rails. This rider is in a good position in the saddle to ensure that her pony is jumping well.

forward, keeping the rhyme and balance for the last three or four strides when he will lengthen his stride and go on with impulsion to clear the fence. You will find you have a good smooth jump, but if you decrease your speed to jump you will find you will go up and down steeply, which is uncomfortable.

Running Out

If your pony ducks out either side of the fence this is known as running out.

Always try to bring your pony into the fence straight. If you approach it at an angle it is inviting him to run out. You will see very experienced riders jumping at angles in eventing and show jumping, but this is too advanced for you at this stage.

If your pony runs out, it generally means you are not in control approaching the fence. Some ponies are wilful, and will set their jaw a few strides before the fence to run out. This type needs strong riding. Try carrying your whip on the side he runs out.

You will find it easier to control your pony at a trot so try again, approaching the lowered fence at a trot. If your pony refuses to go near a fence and naps then you do need expert help.

Remember never to lose your temper with your pony. It never does any good. It will just make you feel terrible and never makes your pony jump. Firm, strong riding is different to losing your temper.

If you feel a battle is approaching, then it is far better to lower the fence, or jump another and plan a schooling day later on with an instructor or experienced friend. Horsey people are always keen to help young riders. Never worry about asking for advice. If they cannot help you themselves, they may well know someone who can.

Hitting the Fence

Most ponies will clear a fence. They do not like to

hurt themselves. If your pony hits fences he may have been overjumped or is finding the ground too hard. Try not to bore him, and rest him from jumping as much as you can for a while. When you restart, approach the fences at a trot so that your pony will be encouraged to round his back and clear the obstacle.

If you constantly jump flimsy fences your pony may get into the habit of hitting them. Avoid flimsy fences for a while and only jump better built jumps. It is tempting to only make flimsy fences while out hacking with your friends, as they do not take so long to build.

Use of a Neckstrap

We strongly recommend the use of a neckstrap or a martingale, when jumping. If you get into the habit of holding the neckstrap with one hand, while still holding the rein in that hand, you will avoid hurting your pony in the mouth by getting left behind when he jumps. Using a neckstrap will give you more confidence. You will see experienced riders using neckstraps when jumping tricky fences cross country.

12 *Tally-ho!*

It is possible to have enormous fun with your pony in an exacting sport without winning a single rosette. In this sport you can enjoy the thrills of riding across natural country, visiting areas which you would not be able to enjoy without being in the saddle. We are referring, of course, to the opportunity to ride your pony in the hunting field. In Britain we are so lucky to have Hunts all over the countryside offering a huge variety of riding experiences. Ponies are capable of following hounds over all kinds of country, although you must be aware of any limitations of your own pony.

In many areas of Britain there are moorland countries which are splendid to ride over and which will enable you to see hounds working easily. Elsewhere you will find the opportunity to ride over privately owned farmland. This is because the Hunts have for so long maintained friendly co-operation with farmers and landowners to take hounds on their land.

This places a big responsibility on all who ride after the hounds to make sure they do not cause damage. The worst errors are to leave open farm gates allowing farm animals to wander, or to ride over growing crops.

Many Pony Clubs are linked to their local Hunts. This is the easiest way for the young rider to enter the hunting field for the first time. The Pony Club and the Hunt arrange special days for children during the Christmas holiday, and the Pony Club will teach you all you need to know about the rules of the hunting field before you set forth.

There are about 200 packs of foxhounds in Britain. Packs of harriers hunting hares are also followed by people on horseback. In the West Country there are packs of Stag hounds on the Devon and Somerset borders which have very large followings of people of all ages, many of them riding ponies. There are packs of Draghounds which do not hunt a live animal, but follow an artificial scent laid by man.

Your pony's natural sure-footedness, hardiness and intelligence are just the qualities which a hunter needs in taking on obstacles of all kinds.

In many areas of the countryside your pony will simply need to jump simple rails, or 'tiger traps', which are built by the Hunt to enable horses and ponies to jump gaps in fences otherwise impossible to leap because they are laced with barbed wire. Ponies are often cleverer than many horses at jumping such specially made hunt jumps. So you need not worry that your pony will not be able to keep you in the hunt.

However, most packs in jumping country have areas which are very strongly fenced and which need all the scope of a large horse to cross them. Your Pony Club will be able to advise you which days are the most suitable to attend on your pony. If you are not a Pony Club member it is still possible to go hunting, but it is vital you have help and guidance from someone experienced. You should not start hunting on your pony unless you are accompanied by someone much older who can guide you and look after you if things go wrong.

Your companion should explain to you what is going on during the day, and should be ready to give you a lead over a jump whenever necessary.

Some Pony Club branches arrange for special escorts for children in the hunting field. Others arrange lessons and tests before children go hunting.

You should make an effort to read something about the hunting field. Here is a brief guide which should help:

The fox is abundant in most of our countryside. Hunting only takes place in the autumn, winter and early spring. For the rest of the year the fox is not hunted with hounds, and the Hunt will make every effort to protect the small copses of woodland in its area where the fox often rears its young. These are called coverts (pronounced covers, you do not sound the 't'). Many other small wild animals live in these coverts, so the Hunt helps to provide a sanctuary for all sorts of wild animals as well as the fox. The small clumps of woodland you will see all over the British countryside did not arrive there by accident; most were planted and maintained there for fox hunting purposes.

Is Fox-hunting Cruel?

You will soon find out if you go hunting regularly that the fox is either killed outright by the hounds if it is caught, or it escapes completely unharmed.

It is not left to die slowly from the injuries which can happen so easily if control of the fox population is attempted with the use of guns, snares, traps or poison.

Why Kill the Fox at All?

Britain has a very large fox population, and there is no natural control of foxes by larger animals in our countryside. Some control is essential to prevent the fox becoming too much of a nuisance in destroying poultry and sheep. The fox itself is a hunter of small animals and birds.

Autumn Hunting

In the autumn, hunting starts early in the morning.

This is called cubhunting, but the fox at that time of year is *not* a furry, little cub; it is fully grown and looks much the same whether it was born the same year, or in previous years.

Much of the hunting in the autumn is within the copses or woodlands. The chase does not take place in the open until later, and this is a good thing because the ground is often hard and dry in late August and September when sport begins. Hounds meet at 7.00 a.m. or even earlier because at this time of year the scent of the fox is much easier for hounds to pick up with their noses when there is a dew on the ground and the air is cool.

You will probably begin your hunting during this cubhunting period which starts in most hunting counties in late August or early September. It is a very good time to start fox hunting for the first time and, hopefully, you will still be on your summer school holidays then.

This is an excellent time for you and your pony to form a good working partnership in the hunting field. There is far less galloping and jumping during cubhunting, and your pony will have a chance to settle down and behave sensibly when out with hounds. Some ponies and horses find hunting all too exciting, but most soon take the experience calmly and thoroughly enjoy themselves.

It is important that your pony is reasonably fit before you take him cubhunting, since early season sport commences so early in the morning and you and your pony will be out with hounds for at least three or four hours. Later, in October, cubhunting commences at 8.00 a.m. and you might be able to go out with the Hunt during your half-term holiday.

You need not plait your pony's mane when you take him cubhunting, but make sure he is as clean and well groomed as possible. This may be difficult as you will not have much time before 7.00 a.m., and you may have to catch him from the field when it is only just getting light. Do the best you can. Your tack should also be clean and in good order because a broken rein, stirrup leather or girth can be disastrous in the hunting field.

For cubhunting you must wear 'Ratcatcher' dress which means your Pony Club riding clothes: a crash hat with black or navy blue covering; collar and tie; tweed hacking jacket; jodhpurs and jodhpur boots; or breeches with plain riding boots.

During cubhunting you may wear a spotted hunting tie instead of an ordinary tie.

We recommend you to use a proper hunting whip with handle and a lash. A hunting whip with a handle is extremely useful in opening and shutting gates, but make sure you practise carrying it, and opening gates, *before* you go out cubhunting.

You approach the gate with your pony's shoulder towards the hinge end whichever that may be. You switch your hunting whip to the hand nearest the gate, and lean forward to pull or lift the gate latch. (Some awkward gates cannot be opened this way and you will have to dismount.) When you have undone the latch make your pony walk round the opening gate, and through the gap. Sometimes it is necessary to hold the gate with the whip handle while you go through, but mostly you will have to turn the pony when you have walked through. You should then lean forward to pull the gate back with your hand or the whip handle, which may also be useful in doing up the latch.

When following other riders through gateways, switch your hunting whip to the hand nearest the gate. Release it and be ready to ward off the gate if it is likely to swing shut on you and your pony. It is all too easy to receive a nasty blow from a swinging gate, and some horses and ponies become nervous in gateways for this reason.

A good hunting pony should always be trained at home to be co-operative and sensible at gateways. It is all too easy to have an accident in gateways and sometimes your pony will catch its reins or martingale in the latch causing it to panic and become more entangled with even more disastrous results.

Always be careful of walking up behind other horses and ponies in gateways. It is a place where some will always kick something approaching quickly from behind.

Hopefully your pony is not a kicker but, if it has any tendency towards this, you should tie a red ribbon in a bow around its upper tail to warn others, and take extra care to ensure that your pony is not in a position to kick. This may mean, alas, that you have to go through gateways behind all the others.

Kicking is a very serious offence anywhere and only cured by instant punishment, so that the pony knows why it is being punished. Children should not ride kickers, but it can sometimes happen that a well-balanced, excited pony will kick, even in the hunting field. If this should happen, immediately take your pony away from the others, and as soon as you can strike it several times behind the saddle, at the same time growling at him severely. Make sure you take a firm hold of the reins so your pony cannot rush suddenly away.

A confirmed kicker will not be cured easily and it may mean that you must strictly limit your activities with it. Probably, you will not be able to take it hunting. It is all too easy to break another rider's leg, damage another pony badly or commit the most awful sin of kicking a hound, which could cause the Master to ask you to go home straight away.

You may travel to the meet in a trailer or horse box, but if possible try to start your hunting season by hacking to the meet if there is one close to your home. Your pony will arrive at the meet in a far more settled condition after a hack, and should be far less inclined to misbehave when it sees hounds for the first time. Some older ponies are well aware

YOUR PONY

A special day's hunting for the Pony Club. Members of the Blackmore and Sparkford Vale branch enjoying their ride after hounds, following a Pony Club meet.

that a pack of hounds means the opportunity to gallop and jump, and they can become somewhat too excited even at the meet.

A good hunter, whether pony or horse, has the temperament to stand quietly for as long as necessary, saving its energy for the action to come when hounds run.

When you arrive at the meet, it is correct to approach the Master, or Masters, and say good morning. The adults will be wearing rat catcher at this time of the year, and you may find it difficult to know which is the Master.

Your Pony Club should have instructed you about

the way your particular Hunt is run before you go hunting.

Remember, the hunstman will be wearing a Hunt coat, probably red, during cubhunting and he will be assisted by one or two whippers-in, similarly dressed. Sometimes the huntsman is an amateur who is also a Master of the Hunt, but very often the huntsman is a full-time professional, not a Master.

One of the Masters will act as Field Master for the day's hunting. A Field Master's task is to lead all the mounted followers, known as the field, when they follow hounds across country. It is important the field do not interfere with the huntsman or hounds, and do not go over any land where crops might be ruined. The Field Master should give a lead over the best route to take.

Sometimes it is difficult to work out who is who, but you should be aware that this is how the Hunt is run, and try and learn who is in charge in the hunting field.

The Hunt Secretary collects the subscriptions, field money and caps for the Hunt. A cap is the money you pay for a day's hunting if you do not subscribe. There are special rates for Pony Club members, varying from £3 to £10. Some Hunts do not charge children whose parents are full subscribers. You will not be required to pay a cap for the early season cubhunting, but by October most Hunts are collecting caps. It is a great help if you find out beforehand from a friend, or your District Commissioner, how much it is, and have the correct amount in your pocket.

The meet for cubhunting may be at a cross-roads, farmyard or some other landmark. Make sure you are there on time, as if you are late you may interfere with the work of the hounds by approaching them cross country just as a fox is running towards you. Heading the fox, or turning it back, will disrupt a hunt, sometimes at the expense of the fox.

The huntsman will take hounds from the cubhunting meet to first covert which will be a small copse or woodland or perhaps a field of kale on a farm, or simply an area of gorse in a moorland country.

If it is a covert in a farming area, the Field Master may ask you and other members of the mounted field to line the areas around the covert. Your task then is to watch for signs of the fox coming out of the cover.

Members of the field may discourage it from leaving the covert by tapping their saddles or boots with their whips, and when past them and well on its way, they will then holla. The huntsman will then bring hounds to the point where the holla was, put it on the line and hunt it across country which in the early part of the season will produce a short scamper.

When you first go cubhunting take the lead of older, more experienced people in assisting the huntsman.

If you make a mistake or holla in the wrong place or at the wrong time you can disrupt the morning's cubhunting.

Do not worry too much about getting this right. Young riders are not expected to play a large part in cubhunting; the best thing you can do is to keep your pony out of trouble.

Use your eyes and ears to watch carefully what is going on and do not chatter too much with your friends or you may miss some of the goings on.

Do not engage in practice jumping if hounds are drawing coverts. Keep your pony well out of the way of the huntsman and hounds, but if hounds happen to approach your pony always turn his head towards them to lessen the chance of him kicking them.

If you do carry a hunting whip you may hold the lash out at arm's length to discourage the hounds from getting too close. On no account crack your whip at the hounds or shout at them.

When hounds are put into the covert by the huntsman they will remain fairly silent until they detect the smell of a fox with their noses. They will then give tongue or 'speak' and you will hear the glorious sound of hounds in full cry as they run up and down the covert in pursuit of the fox or foxes.

Your pony may get excited at this time, so be ready to calm him or move him further away from the covert.

The Hunting Season

The hunting season proper starts on 1 November, and the opening meets are held near that date.

If you have been cubhunting regularly, the start of the season should hold no special problems for you, but remember that the aim now is to hunt in the open.

The mounted followers wait until the fox and the pursuing hounds are running out of the covert, across country, before endeavouring to follow them.

Follow the lead of the Field Master across country. It is vital that you should be able to control the speed of your pony. If you have no 'brakes' you should not be in the hunting field. Keep your pony at the pace set by the Field Master and the experienced riders at the front of the field. If you are in a jumping county do not attempt to jump anything you know is beyond you and your pony's abilities. There are plenty of rails, 'tiger traps' and perhaps small hedges which you and your pony can manage, but do practise clearing such obstacles elsewhere before you try them in the hunting field. Pony Club Hunter Trials offer marvellous experience of the sort of jumps you will meet out hunting.

Here are some useful tips to keep you out of trouble, and to increase your fun:

Do not unbox very close to the meet. Hack to the meet to settle your pony down before you get there.

At the meet watch out for other horses' and ponies' hind legs. Do not barge about and risk getting kicked. Keep well clear of hounds, but if hounds approach you, always turn your pony's head towards them to avoid any risk of your pony kicking a hound.

On roads and lanes take care to avoid the slippery patches. If there is a ridable grass verge use it instead of the road surface.

On farmland do not ride over growing crops; keep well into the side in single file if the Field Master takes you round the edge of crops. On grass, keep well clear of farm cattle and sheep; avoid stampeding them by not galloping close to them.

If you are last through a gateway you must see that it is closed and latched behind you.

There are often queues of horses and ponies at jumps. When it is your turn, give the rider in front time to land and get well clear before you follow. At all costs avoid jumping on to the horse in front; if the rider has had a fall you could land on him.

Above all, watch the hounds carefully all day. Do not stand chattering and giggling while hounds are working. Listen for the voices of the hounds when they have found a fox and learn to recognize the main calls on the horn sounded by the huntsman, especially 'Gone Away', which are the thrilling notes signalling the start of a hunt.

Learn to ride your pony according to the ground surface and the ups and downs of the countryside. Nurse his strength; do not gallop him up hills unnecessarily, nor expect him to go at speed over very stony, rutted ground. Look after him, and he will be able to look after you.

When jumping fences in the hunting field ride boldly – throw your heart over first – but with common sense. On the far side of a hedge there is often a ditch, so kick on so that your pony can clear hedge *and* ditch safely.

Jump timber much more slowly, but with plenty of impulsion. You may jump over ditches slowly; give your pony plenty of rein, grab your neckstrap or breastplate strap and kick. He can jump very wide ditches almost from a standstill. Never hesitate to grab the strap wherever you feel unsafe. It's far better than hanging on to the reins to stay on.

Do not sit far forward when jumping out hunting. The ground may be rutted on your landing and if your pony stumbles you want to avoid falling over his head.

If you hunt regularly you will improve your seat and your hands and you will greatly improve your partnership with your pony in the flat and over fences.

Good hunting!

13 Cross-country Fun

Hunter Trials

Hunter trials give you and your pony a chance to ride across country in competition against others. You will tackle a varied course, one at a time. The obstacles you meet range from timber to hedges and perhaps ditches. Sometimes the course is situated on a hill, so there may be fences up and downhill with drops.

Hunter trials are great fun and a good way to get experience across country. If you feel your age class is beyond your standard and makes you feel nervous you can ask if you can have a go in a lower class on a non-competitive basis. When you can complete your first course you will soon have the confidence and experience to tackle other classes.

The Day Before

You will be able to walk the course on your feet the day before most hunter trials. This gives you the chance to inspect closely what you have to jump – and worry about it all night.

It is important to walk up to each fence as though you are on your pony, and work out how you will approach the fence. Some fences are straightforward, but others will be at an angle or perhaps near a sharp turn. Try to remember the order of the fences, as everything happens much quicker on the day, and it is easy to lose your way and be eliminated.

CROSS-COUNTRY FUN

At home you must get everything organized for your pony and yourself. It is easier to get your pony clean if he is stabled overnight. You cannot do much about a pony plastered in wet mud on the morning of a hunter trial, but not everyone is lucky enough to have the use of a stable.

Whether your pony is at grass or stabled, it is sensible to check him over, paying special attention to his feet. Shoes must be on firmly because the mud will sometimes pull them off, and if this occurs during the cross-country ride it can split the hoof.

You should make sure your tack is clean and in good order, and pack any rugs and boots your pony will wear. Even if your pony does not wear a martingale it is a good idea to use a neckstrap. Make sure everything is properly sorted out the night before – it makes everything run smoother on the day.

Your riding clothes should be ready for action for the next day. The correct dress for hunter trialling is a hacking jacket, jodhpurs and jodhpur boots, or breeches and hunting boots, crash hat (with hairnet for girls), shirt and tie or hunting tie ('stock' as it is sometimes called). Make sure your crash helmet is of BSI safety standard, carrying the kite mark and number 4472.

Working Hunter Ponies line up in the 15 hh. class at the Royal International Horse Show.

YOUR PONY

Pony Club members should wear their special ties and badges. Gloves and stick complete everything. Body protectors are now often compulsory at hunter trials, and they are a very sensible protection, easily worn under a hacking jacket.

Silks, or colours as they are called in racing, are sometimes worn for the cross-country phase of eventing and some young riders prefer to wear them for hunter trialling too. They are more fun and your friends and family can see you more clearly on the course. This is perfectly all right, except at some hunter trials where the schedule insists hunting dress must be worn, in which case you should use a dark blue or black covering on your crash hat.

Finally, make sure you take sufficient money with the entry form if you have not sent it by post beforehand; remember the schedule and set your alarm clock to allow plenty of time to get to the course well before your class. On hunter trial day everything takes much longer than you imagined.

Before You Leave

Feed your pony as early as possible, even if he is at grass, as it will be quite a long day – and make sure you have a good breakfast, even though you may have butterflies in your stomach.

Give your pony a quick groom although he should be reasonably clean from the previous day. Check his shoes and pick out his feet. It is not necessary to plait the mane for hunter trials, but you will see that most competitors are nicely turned out with well pulled manes and tails. Put on a tail bandage, and tack up if you are hacking to the course.

If you have transport for the pony, pack all the kit in the horse box or trailer, including a haynet for the journey home. You should take grooming kit, first-aid materials, rugs and bandages, a bucket plus water container, as this is not always available, and a

CROSS-COUNTRY FUN

To avoid risking damage to your pony in transit it is wise to use leg guards as shown here. They can be worn over stable bandages and are easily kept in place with Velcro fastenings. This pony has a tail guard attached to the roller over the tail bandage and he is wearing a summer sheet. His owner is walking up the centre of the ramp looking into the trailer to give her pony a confident lead in loading up.

small feed. A picnic with thermos are essential items as well.

If you are hacking to the course you have to limit what to take, but a head collar, and rug if your pony is clipped, are vital, unless these can go in a car.

The weather during the hunter trials season can be windy and wet, so a good selection of waterproofs is a must as several changes of clothing may be necessary.

Arriving at the Course

The first thing to do is to find the Secretary's tent or caravan and enter for your class, unless you have entered by post, in which case, all you have to do is collect your number. At hunter trials these are usually large, bib-style eventing numbers which can be clearly seen. Sometimes you have to leave a cash deposit for the number so the organizers can make sure they get them all back.

There will be a plan of the course at the Secretary's office, so work out the route for your class. Remember that at all times white flags are on the left, and red flags on the right. The classes vary slightly, and where there are different routes and fences the flags will be changed. Unless you are in the first class think ahead and remember the changes.

The lowest fences are usually in the first class for the novice and junior sections. There is sometimes a separate course for mini-hunter trials for riders aged nine and under, or ages nine to eleven; these fences should be low, and the course short and easy.

Do not overface your pony. If you feel the fences in your class are beyond your standard, you can always ask if you can compete in a lower class.

Your pony will need a good warm-up and practice jump, but don't wear him out before you start. Once round the course is quite enough for most ponies unless they are very fit, but you might decide to ride additionally in the pairs class. This class is fun and it is ideal for getting your pony going. However, the pace can become fast when riding in a pair so do make sure you will not be out of control. Even the quietest pony can become surprisingly competitive when jumping alongside another.

Some ponies do need a stronger bit than the one you use for ordinary hacking. A hunter trial reminds some ponies of hunting, and they all love galloping across fields. My daughter's present pony has a plain snaffle for hacking, showing and rallies, but she uses a kimblewick for hunter trialling.

Preparing to Ride the Course

About ten minutes before you are due to start, ride your pony down to the start area, and report to the starter or assistant. You will then be told how many more competitors there are starting before you. Now is the time to have a practice jump.

Two or three times over the practice jump as a warm-up is enough for both of you. Try to carry this out as you would in a hunter trial by making a slightly longer run-in at something near a hunting pace. On landing, canter off further than you would if you were show jumping.

The height of the practice jump should be the same as the fences on the course, an easy, inviting fence with ground line or cross poles. The aim of the practice fence is to give confidence to you and your pony, as well as sharpening up the pony before the real thing.

Walk your pony around near the start until you are told to start the course. Do remember to check your girths and stirrups in plenty of time, not forgetting putting your gloves on, and making sure you are ready for action. Your attitude will be conveyed to the pony – so ensure that you are concentrating on a good start.

Riding the Course

When you start, settle as soon as possible into a steady pace. It is not necessary to gallop very fast from the beginning. Competitors who do this are mainly showing off, or perhaps out of control.

Very few courses are nowadays timed against the clock all the way round, as this has proved far too hazardous. Usually there is a timed section midway on the course, comprising about five or six fences. You should conserve your pony's energy for this part of the course. Sometimes the section is judged on style, which I much prefer, so it is essential to keep your pony at a good steady hunting pace, ensuring that you maintain correct position in the saddle between the obstacles and when you are jumping.

The ideal speed is a fast canter, not a flat out gallop, and you should always feel your pony has more speed in reserve. You should keep contact with his mouth, the degree depending on how much of a 'hold', or how strong, he is. Your position in the saddle should be slightly forward, to make the ride easier for him and better balanced for you.

The first few fences will probably be straightforward but your pony will know he is going away from the other ponies, and may take a while to get into his stride. So do not take any fence for granted. Present your pony properly and use your legs. It is vital to make your pony concentrate on the course and the fences. Be ready for a lack of resolution over the early fences.

Tree trunks, oil drums and straw bales with timber poles, sleepers and brush fences are often among the obstacles on the first part of the course, so make sure you have practised over such jumps well-beforehand at home.

CROSS-COUNTRY FUN

When approaching a fence it is important to balance your pony about four or five strides away, by checking the pace slightly, sitting down in the saddle, and using your legs to send your pony on and over the fence. You should always maintain contact with the mouth so that your pony does not run or duck out. You should always look up and over the fence as you approach and jump it. If you are unduly worried about the course, or an individual fence, this will always be communicated to your pony, and he may become worried too. So you must always be positive, and think you are going to get over. Throw your heart over first. Never think you will fall off. As we said before, if you are seriously worried when you walk the course, enter for a lower height course.

Further on in the course you may meet a drop fence. Try not to think about this too much, as

ponies all jump them naturally. The only thing to remember is to sit back as you land, and put your legs forward so that you do not get jumped off. This gets much easier with experience, but remember that you want a smooth jump, not an 'up and down' jump as this makes the fence seem much bigger. Send your pony on, well into the fence, and slip the reins slightly on landing, so that you are not pulled off by them.

Children are fortunate if they live in hunting counties where they get experience of jumping drop fences from an early age. Drops do not generally cause problems to the ponies – only to the riders.

Ditches tend to cause more problems. A ditch in front of a fence may produce trouble at hunter trials if you have not schooled over such a combination beforehand. Ponies should be well-used to them and jump the ditch as though it was not there. Inexperienced ponies tend to see the ditch suddenly at the last moment, look into it and stop suddenly or put in an awkward jump. Schooling is the key to this, and if your pony does not like a ditch then try and get him to follow a bolder pony over first.

Open water may also cause great problems. Ponies are either bold over water or they hate it. At hunter

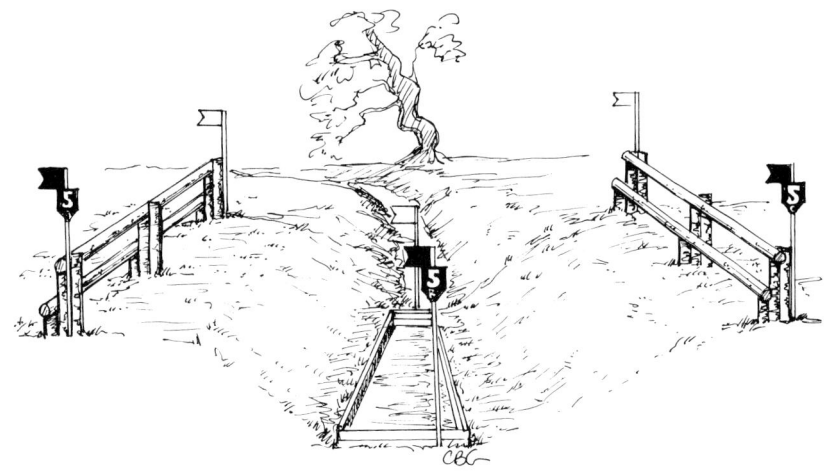

trials where there is open water, it can affect the results tremendously. Again, schooling is the key, by making sure your pony will jump over, or into it, beforehand. True hunting ponies have no problems here, but ponies who have not been taught about water when young, often fear it. If your pony is one of these, try to follow someone else into water and stand about in the water until he is well used to it. You need time and patience, but keep persevering. Above all, avoid a battle. Use your legs and heels, not your whip when schooling into water.

When you are approaching water, ride steadily so your pony does not see it suddenly at the last moment, and then send him on strongly. It is great fun on a good pony.

Stiles and gates need a steady, straight approach in order to jump them properly. It is better to show-jump these, as they do not ride quite like other cross-country fences. Take extra care that your pony is well balanced, and jump carefully but with plenty of impulsion.

Occasionally, you will be asked to open a gate, particularly if there is a timed section. It is surprising how long this takes some competitors. However, there are all too many cases where ponies do not understand that they have to stop to open it, and they jump it by mistake. This is a disappointing way of being eliminated. Give your pony proper signals that he is to stop, and even talk him to 'whoa' or 'steady'. Some riders approach the gate from the side if they think their pony will be too keen.

When jumping uphill you will find you have to increase impulsion more before the fence; that is, send on your pony more before the fence keeping the rhyme and balance, so that the rise in ground is allowed for. The reverse is true for fences downhill, when you will find you have to steady more, so that you do not go too fast.

If your pony becomes puffed, give him a breather by slowing down for a while. A track through a wood or some uneven ground are ideal places to let him ease up before you continue at hunting pace. You will find he has more energy for the rest of the course.

The homeward part of the course is generally

CROSS-COUNTRY FUN

straightforward, as you have probably jumped the most difficult fences, and your pony knows he is returning to other ponies. However, you may be getting tired as well, so keep to your pace, and do not let him get too fast.

After the Ride

Get off your pony and slacken the girths before you walk him round to cool off. Later on, when he is dry, you can offer him some water, and let him graze, or put him away in the horse box with a haynet. His rugs should be correct for the temperature of the day. I have seen ponies on freezing days with just a sweat sheet, and ponies rugged-up on very warm days.

You may be thrilled with him and waiting

Georgina and Huckleberry taking a full-sized natural cut-and-laid hunting fence during the local hunter trials. Fences like this must be attacked boldly to ensure the pony jumps them cleanly.

anxiously for the results, but if you know you need further schooling after a disappointing round, you may find someone there who will give you some help in the future, or perhaps even give you some tuition on the course at the end of the day. Some organizers will permit this.

Sponsored Rides

Sponsored rides are a fairly new idea in riding cross country. The course is usually long, from five miles sometimes up to twenty miles, with varying heights and types of fences.

When you enter you have to get sponsored to ride. This involves asking your family and friends to sponsor you for so much a fence, or so much a mile ridden. The proceeds generally go to a Hunt, Pony Club or some charity.

Sponsored rides are not really competitions; they are just a pleasant way of riding and jumping cross-country. The organizers start the competitors in twos or fours, or sometimes groups. The pace is

Georgina and Mini relaxing during a Pony Club event.

much slower than hunter trialling, because of the distance, and you can decide this for yourself. It is best to walk, trot and canter depending on when your pony needs to be rested, but there is seldom any galloping.

These rides are a good way of getting used to your pony in crossing natural country, and trying different fences. They are held in the spring and autumn, and they are usually very popular, so make sure you enter early.

It is not necessary to walk the course. You will find there are mainly two or three options in jumping each fence; they are straightforward, and you can decide which height to jump as you go round. There is never a time factor, you just have to complete the course during the day. It is a relaxed and enjoyable way of cross-country riding.

Pony Club Eventing

Eventing comprises three phases: dressage, cross country and show jumping. Pony Club eventing is a one-day event. For more advanced eventing the phases are spread over two or three days. The winner is the rider with the best score overall from the three phases. Cross country for the pony rider is similar to the hunter trialling we have described, and we discuss show jumping in Chapter 14.

Dressage

Many young riders are daunted by the dressage phase which is always first. Do not be dismayed. If you have schooled your pony properly he should be mannered and on the bit. You should have no difficulty in basic dressage schooling at this level of eventing.

Learn the dressage test thoroughly. You will be told the exact number of your test on the schedule. Pace the test on your feet at home until you know it off by heart. You will have enough to concentrate on during the test trying to get your pony going well, without frantically having to remember the test.

An accurate test is important. You must change direction and pace exactly at the marker indicated. If you are not accurate you will lose marks.

Do not worry if you think you are making a mess of the test. If things go wrong remember you are marked out of ten marks for each section. You may get a low mark for one section, but try to recover for the next section in which you can make up some marks.

You would be wise to watch the previous tests to help keep the test fresh in your mind. Wait until the bell or car horn signals you to enter the arena. You will be given your times from the secretary for each phase which will give you sufficient time to change and prepare your pony.

The scores are written on a large blackboard. Do not get too despondent if you find you are way down the list of results. The lowest score at dressage is the best as the scores are subtracted from a total at the end. These placings can rapidly change after the cross-country phase, and again after the show jumping.

Dressage judges write comments on the results. Try to learn from these to improve your test next time. Show your test sheet to your instructor. You may find it necessary to practise certain parts.

My daughter was told recently by her instructor that her dressage test looked as if she was just out for a hack around the arena! This meant she should gather her horse together and use more impulsion to produce a better test.

Some ponies are used to doing dressage, and they make it much easier for you. Strong ponies are difficult to ride and require calming. You may have to settle them for some time by riding in quietly before your test. Ponies can get bored with too much schooling, so try to understand your pony and his moods.

Ponies may shy at the white boards surrounding the dressage arena if they are not used to them. You may be able to practise in a proper dressage arena with markers before your eventing day. This will help greatly.

If you take your dressage seriously and enjoy it, you will find your pony will become a better ride, and more obedient. This will help your riding and reflect well in your cross country and show jumping.

It will be an advantage if you obtain the Pony Club publication for eventing. This stipulates the tack that your pony is permitted to wear for the various phases. You should wear a tweed hacking jacket and tie for the dressage, colours for cross country and then your hacking jacket and tie for show jumping. You should have a body protector, and a proper crash helmet is compulsory.

14 Show Time

Horse Shows

Many young riders spoil their chances of winning rosettes at Horse Shows by not being properly organized. There are sometimes five or six different rings at horse shows with various competitions taking place throughout the day. If you intend to ride in several classes it needs planning to make sure you arrive at each one on time and well prepared.

The main ring, or ring one, is usually for show jumping classes; ring two is often for working hunter classes with natural rustic fences; and rings three and four for showing classes. There may be a separate gymkhana ring, a handy pony competition ring and a ring for minimus clear round jumping.

We discuss the competitions later in the chapter but you can see that you have to choose your classes carefully, enter in good time and prepare your pony and yourself.

All too often, classes do not run to time, so you should check what is happening in other rings. Be ready to walk the jumping courses; get to the collecting ring, the small roped area your pony will go into before entering the ring, before your class; make sure you are back in time for a jump-off; and then for the presentations of the prizes if you have been successful.

Some young riders get flustered at horse shows, and rush about from ring to ring without knowing the course, and with ponies badly turned out and presented. Sometimes they do not even allow time for a practice jump before going into the ring.

Classes in different rings can clash, so it is important to be well organized. Do not try to compete in too many different classes. If your parents or friends are at the show they may be able to help you plan, make entries for you and call you over to the ring when it is your turn to jump. Many children, however, go to shows on their own, and until they are more experienced, it can be difficult to organize themselves.

When I am judging I often see competitors rushing about at the last moment before the class. In working-hunter pony classes some riders come into the ring to jump without having given themselves sufficient time to study the fences beforehand. It takes quite a time to tack up, get your kit ready and find your number. Too many riders leave all this until about five minutes before they are due in the ring.

If there are many entries in, for example, a novice jumping class, to save waiting about for ages in the collecting ring put your number down on the collecting ring board early. The steward there makes up a list of the order of jumping, so he will have the next two or three ponies waiting their turn to jump. It is best not to wait too long in the collecting ring or your pony may not want to leave the other ponies. All too often one sees ponies stopping or refusing as soon as they enter the jumping ring for this reason.

It is better not to go amongst the first few to jump unless you are an experienced rider. If you watch a couple of competitors jump the course you may gain some insight into how the course rides. Look out for difficult corners and spooky fences. Watching others should also help you remember the course.

So while you are waiting for your turn, watch the other competitors in the ring most carefully. Try to imagine how you could ride the fences better. It is valuable experience to watch all levels of riding to see either how it should be done, or how it could be improved.

If you have never competed at a horse show it is a good idea to go mainly as a spectator the first time; perhaps just compete in the minimus jumping class. You will learn a great deal about the standard of the other competitors, and how classes are judged, which should help you when you compete.

If you become keen on competing at your local shows you may be tempted to give your pony a heavy programme of such work in the summer holidays. No two ponies are the same, but remember that many get tired at the end of a long day. Do not sit on your pony all day at the show, treating him as a viewing position when you do not need to ride him. Dismount, ease the girths, sponge the sweat stains off him, give him water, stand him in the shade, and give him a pick of grass to help him relax between classes. Above all, do not gallop about madly all day long; you will be a nuisance to everyone else and you will be unkind to your pony.

However careful of his welfare you may be, your pony may become jarred by working on hard going in the summer. Even the most genuine, willing pony may become sour, unco-operative and begin refusing at jumps. The solution is to sweeten him up with a short rest, even if this means going to fewer shows during your school holidays.

You will enjoy horse shows best if you remember that you are doing it for fun. Winning caps and rosettes is fine, but do so in partnership with your pony, not at the expense of his health and well-being. He is not a machine to enable you to go pot-hunting.

Preparation for Showing Classes

Most young riders love jumping classes but you should not overlook the showing classes. They offer so many varied opportunities. There are show-hunter pony classes, show pony classes, mountain and moorland

SHOW TIME

Show Hunter Pony: a nice example of hunter pony with good action. In this picture he is pulling and overbent making him a more difficult ride. He will loose marks for this as it is a serious fault in the hunting field.

novice pony, local riders, and in hand classes for young stock. If you want a showing class with more action, a working-hunter pony class includes jumping a set of fences made to look as natural as possible, with rustic timber and brush fences similar to those you could meet in a day's hunting.

Do not be put off by showing classes. Watch them first and then try and show your pony properly to the best advantage. There are only a few top-level ponies at the big shows, and a moderate pony can do well if it is produced and schooled well.

Some owners often wonder why their expensive ponies do not win. If your pony is not in good condition and not properly shown it will finish down the line or even in the back row, no matter how well-bred, or how much money has been paid for it.

If you persevere with showing you will find in time that your efforts will be rewarded in other ways as well as by possible rosettes and cups. Because you

are making an extra effort to keep your pony looking its best, your pony will look smart for hacking and Pony Club rallies. You will have learned to pay special attention to grooming and turnout.

Schooling the pony will improve your riding and your pony will benefit too. Working hunter competitions will enhance your jumping, and your enjoyment of hacking and hunting. Too many young riders never know what it is like to ride a well-schooled pony. If your own is not well schooled, try having a riding lesson on a pony that is in this class, so that you know what it feels like and what you are aiming for.

Keeping your tack up to showing standards will ensure your saddlery is kept supple and lasts longer. This is sensible, because saddles and bridles are increasingly expensive.

You will also become more aware of all the ailments and unsoundnesses that would affect your pony's showing performance. Showing also makes you take extra care over feeding and conditioning. Judges choose winners who look good in their coats, and are clearly well kept.

Above all showing is character building. Never forget to smile; look as if you are enjoying yourself. Sometimes a child who looks disagreeable and bad tempered is riding a difficult pony, but often the pony is wonderful and the child is just feeling out of sorts or nervous. Do try and smile and look happy and relaxed, and this will certainly improve the overall picture. It will also help your mental attitude, and encourage your pony to go better for you.

Every pony, and horse, has an extraordinary ability to tune into the mood and attitude of the rider. A positive, confident temperament on the part of the rider helps a lot in producing the same from the mount. This is partly why horses and ponies perform so much better for certain riders. Sheer riding skill is only part of the story.

Trimming

Since it is obviously important your pony looks his best at a show, you must have him groomed and trimmed neatly. This is a fairly simple and easy procedure, but nearly all ponies in showing classes could look *much* neater.

Opposite: *superb Show and Working Hunter Pony, Chideock Strongbow ridden by Christopher Ryder-Phillips, wearing his Championship rosettes at Hickstead's Nations Cup meeting.*

Trimming your pony effectively makes all the difference in the distribution of the rosettes at the end of the class.

Mane

A nicely pulled mane and forelock is best achieved gradually. First, the withers have to be trimmed, but only shorten the mane about an inch or two where it would go under the saddle and the area just in front of the saddle where your hands would rub. Do not make the mistake of trimming too far up the mane from this end.

Next deal with the mane under the headpiece; just behind the pony's ears. Put on a bridle to measure both these areas; you should trim the mane close with clippers or scissors.

Pulling a mane is not difficult, but it is a knack you can learn with practice. Some ponies have such thick manes that they cannot be plaited properly without pulling.

The first rule is never to use scissors. Rely on the mane comb; the best ones are the smaller variety, with close teeth.

You are endeavouring to produce an even, thinned mane of about four to five inches long, laying on the offside of the neck.

Hold the ends of a small piece of mane in your left hand between your thumb and first finger. Then with your right hand comb the pieces back to the required length. Comb back the shorter piece of mane, and break off the longer pieces you are holding. Use the comb to break the hair or you will cut your finger. If the pony has a very long mane you can wrap the mane around the comb, which helps to pull it out. Be careful not to pull the mane much shorter than four to five inches. Repeat the process along the whole length of the mane. If you are left handed, reverse the above directions.

At your first attempt, only pull part of the mane as

this is a lengthy procedure for the novice and your pony can get very restive. Some ponies may resist very strongly and in these cases you will need expert adult help. It is best to start pulling a pony's mane on returning from a ride, as the skin is then warm, and this makes the hair come out easier.

If your pony's mane lies naturally to the near side (left side), you will have to turn it over with a wet brush, and then either plait it or bunch it in plaits, with elastic bands until it stays over naturally.

Ponies suffering from the condition sweet itch sometimes have their manes hogged; that is, clipped off, and this should be clipped when it is starting to grow. Scissors will not produce a good finish as they make it too difficult to get the mane even.

Tails

A nicely pulled tail can give a pony the illusion of having much improved hind quarters and thereby improve the animal's quality when being judged. When pulling the tail it is again best to carry this out in several stages. Pull the hair out from the sides, but do not pull too much as you will get bald patches! Use the mane comb to break off the hairs.

The aim is to achieve a tail which flows smoothly – and appears to be all of one piece, with no hairs sticking out in untidy gashes. When you are beginning to get the right shape, use a sponge to damp it and then bandage the top of the tail, so that you can see which hairs to pull out next.

The length of the tail to be achieved is ideally about four inches below the hock. You may now use scissors to cut the tail to the overall length from the bottom. Cut gradually until you are sure you have the correct length. Remember a pony carries his tail higher when moving, so do not cut off too much.

Extra Trimming

You should trim your pony's ears by pressing the lobes

together lengthwise and cutting out the extra hairs which will then protrude. Scissors are suitable for this task, unless you are clipping the whole head, in which case you can use clippers carefully on the ears as well. Some ponies need trimming around the jaw line; facial whiskers are best cut off around the muzzle.

Heels should be trimmed in the summer for showing, and clippers are best, but alternatively scissors may be used with a comb, rather in the way your own hair is cut. Work carefully to avoid leaving a jagged edge of hair around the heel.

If your pony lives out in winter, you should leave the heels unclipped at that time of the year. Rainwater runs off the hair which acts as a valuable protection for the heels, so let the hair grow out after the showing season.

When you are trimming the higher parts, you may have difficulty reaching, so use a bucket or stool to stand on. Ponies soon get used to this, and you can see what you are doing then without your arms aching.

Plaiting

If your pony has a nicely pulled mane it is easy to plait. There should always be an uneven number of plaits down the neck, plus the forelock. The most usual number is seven down the crest, making eight with the forelock.

You can plait with thread or rubber bands. Sewing always looks better, and thread does not take much longer than rubber bands.

You will need: a water brush; a strong, blunt needle with a large eye; plaiting thread bought at a saddlers to match the colour of your pony's mane (ordinary cotton is difficult to use as it is not strong enough); mane comb; and scissors.

Damp the mane with the water brush, and divide it up into parts with rubber bands. This helps you plan where to plait.

SHOW TIME

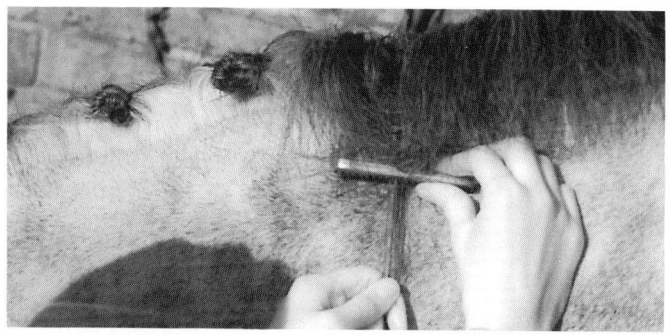
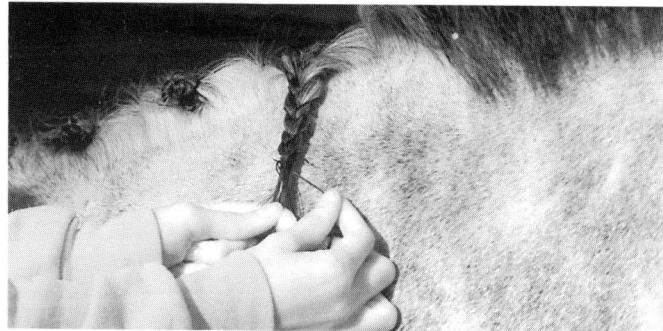
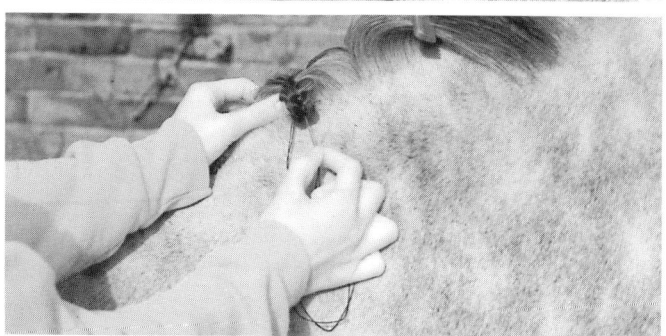
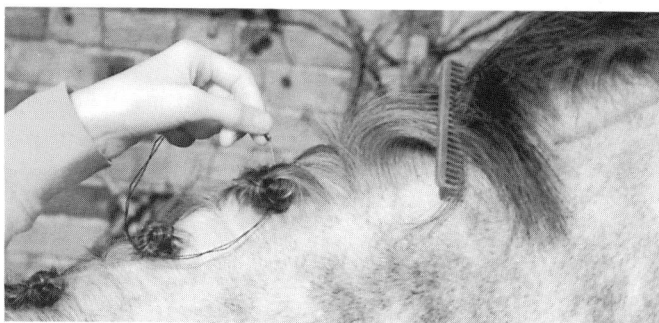

Plaiting: hold the end of a small piece of mane between thumb and first finger of the left hand. Comb the hair back to about four or five inches. Break off the longer pieces you are holding. Divide the mane into seven sections and dampen with a water brush. Start plaiting at the top and work down. When the plait is complete firmly secure the end with thread. Double the plait under; push the needle through from underneath close to the crest, pull the thread through and repeat. Double the plait again and repeat. Cut the thread off from the underside.

Start to plait by making sure you plait tightly at the crest (top) end. When the plait is complete, firmly secure the end with the thread. It should not unravel at this stage. Double the end of the plait under, push the needle through the plait from the underneath to close to the crest. Pull the thread through, and then push the needle through the plait again. Double up the plait again and repeat.

You may need to push the thread through several times to secure it firmly, and even loop the thread around each side of the plait from the middle. Cut the thread off from the underside, and trim any protruding hairs.

Always be careful not to cut into the mane, or cut chunks out, especially when you take out the plaits.

If you use rubber bands, make sure you pull them tightly. It is best to use two rubber bands on each plait in case one breaks when you are riding.

Mane plaits should not be left in at night as they pull the mane causing it to break.

Show Jumping

At larger horse shows the show jumping classes are affiliated to the British Show Jumping Association (BSJA). This means you are not allowed to enter unless you are a member. Generally the standard is high. The junior classes are for ages sixteen and under on ponies 14.2 hh. and less. You may decide you wish to specialize and attempt to achieve this standard.

Show jumping at smaller shows is open to anyone, and the schedule will state the different classes. These include novice show jumping for horses and ponies not having won a first prize, junior classes of 12.2 hh. and under and 14.2 hh. and under.

Sometimes the height of the pony will also include the age of the rider, for example ponies 12.2 hh. and under, and riders aged eleven and under. There are usually classes to suit everyone of varying ages, heights of pony and ability.

There may be a speed class usually the scurry where the fastest clear round wins. In other classes, the clear rounds go forward to the jump-off. The jump-off is sometimes timed, the fastest winning, or there may be a second jump-off over a shortened raised course.

No marks are given for style in show jumping. There are penalties for errors at fences:

MISTAKE	*PENALTY*
knocking down a fence	4 faults
first refusal	3 faults
second refusal in whole round	6 faults
third refusal in whole round	elimination
fall of horse or rider	8 faults

There may be a time allowed for the course, so you must finish within the time. Do not worry too much about this. It will only penalize you if you trot slowly all the way. At larger shows it becomes more important to keep within the time limit.

You must also make sure you go through the start and finish markers, or you will be eliminated.

If there is a double and you stop at the second part, you must go back and jump both parts again.

You must learn the course well, so that you can steer your pony round it. When you first start show jumping you may find this hard, but it will become easier with practice. It can be nerve racking to go into the ring with everyone watching.

Clear Round Show Jumping (Minimus Jumping)

Most horse shows today have a clear round jumping ring. This is an ideal way to start. You pay your entrance money at the ring and then have a go. If you go clear you receive a rosette. If you have any problems you can have another attempt.

There is no winner, and the jumps are usually raised during the day. If you decide to go again make sure your pony has his breath back. It is unfair to ask him to keep going round; he will only get bored.

For more experienced riders it can be a good way of getting their ponies going before entering the jumping classes. My daughter always likes the clear round jumping. If the fences are lower than usual she will go round without stirrups which is good practise for her riding.

Handy Pony Class

Again, this is in a separate ring. You and your pony will be timed round a number of hazards. This is fun but it needs practising at home. You will have to dismount and remount and the hazards will include putting washing on a line; pushing a wheelbarrow; leading your pony; walking between sacks or markers; reining back through hay bales; and whatever else they have thought up. Your pony might not like the look of some of it, but with practice you can get quicker. The winner must have the fastest round throughout the day.

Showing Classes

There is a good variety of showing classes at local shows. 'Best Turned Out' is for the best pony and rider in smart appearance. You are only required to walk and perhaps trot in the ring; the rest of the time you line up for the inspection. Everything should be immaculate. If you have never taken your pony in the ring with others before, this can be a good class in which to start.

Showing classes are sometimes judged on the pony, at other times the best rider. They are divided into heights and ages. You will ride round the ring together at a walk, trot and canter, and then you will be called into the centre by the judge's steward. You will be asked to give a solo show, which is a two-minute display around the ring. You should walk, trot, canter and gallop if asked, on both legs, with a change of direction, and then come to a collected halt bowing to the judge. Watch the experienced competitors and see how they perform. Do not walk for too long; trot in a figure of eight and then canter, going wide around the ring before halting.

While watching the other riders, plan exactly where you will change pace and direction. To gain good marks your show should be accurate, polished and controlled. It is all too easy to let it become aimless, ragged and boring. Practise at home. There is quite an art in giving a good show. Look as if you are enjoying yourself and smile. You may feel nervous and worried, but try not to show it. A judge likes to see a happy, confident rider who looks as if he or she is enjoying the ride.

You may be asked to take the saddle off your pony and stand him out before the judge, so that his conformation can be judged. His movement is then assessed by walking and trotting him out. We have discussed this in Chapter 2 on buying a pony.

At the end of the class you should walk round in a small circle when the prize winners are called in. Do not be disheartened if you do not win a rosette. Keep learning to see how you could improve; it is not that impossible.

Working Pony Classes

Working pony classes are divided into 13 hh., 14 hh. and 15 hh. sections. The riders' ages are sometimes

The performance part of a Working Hunter Pony class. This combination is going well round the course at the Royal International Horse Show in the grounds of the National Exhibition Centre, Birmingham.

divided: 13 hh. with fourteen years and under; 14 hh. with sixteen years and under; and 15 hh. with eighteen years and under.

There are two smaller classes for younger riders; the cradle stakes is for ponies 12 hh. and under and riders nine years and under; and the nursery stakes is for ponies 13 hh. and under and riders eleven years and under.

In these competitions you are required to jump rustic courses similar to fences you would meet out hunting. The jumping phase is judged on style, and differs from show jumping. Working-hunter pony style must be fluent and even paced, with impulsion before the fences. Judges are looking for the style you would use cross country, but obviously more controlled for a show ring. The whole round should be pleasing to the eye, and ideally your aids should be invisible.

The clear round competitors come back into the

ring, and the class is judged in the manner of a show class.

Working pony classes are a good way of starting showing. If your pony jumps well you find you have a chance of a rosette as most judges consider this phase the most important part of the class.

British Show Pony Society

Some shows have BSPS show classes, and this means the classes are judged under their rules. Small local shows are generally not under BSPS rules, but do not be put off if your show is affiliated. If your pony and you are capable of jumping the course, you will not be outclassed. The course may include a ditch and substantially built fences, but if your pony jumps well you will be fine.

Gymkhana Events

At most horse shows there is a gymkhana ring which sometimes operates all the afternoon. You will soon find out how speedy your pony is. You may find your pony has obviously done this all before, and is keen. Thus you can have a good time in gymkhana events. Most ponies can be trained with time and practice to be competent gymkhana ponies.

Some ponies do not like gymkhana events, so do not overdo them. Be selective in the number of classes you enter to stop your pony becoming bored.

If you feel your pony is getting out of control by racing against other ponies you will have to restrain and steady him. It is dangerous to go too fast as you may have a bad fall. Ponies that will not wait for you to mount before racing off can be particularly dangerous.

Getting a good start at the 'off' can gain you several lengths. Practise at home so that you are adept at taking potatoes off poles and manoeuvring flags.

In the smallest age classes the ponies can be

led. It is much better to lead a pony so that a young child gains confidence.

There are many events, and the ring stewards will call out the rules before the class telling you exactly what to do. If there are a lot of competitors, each class is run in heats, the winners going forward to the finals.

The **bending race** requires an agile, fast pony. There is a line of poles which you have to go between as fast as possible, turning round the end one, and weaving back again. You will be eliminated if you knock down a pole or miss one out.

In the **potato race** the rider can only use one hand on the reins, as the potato has to be carried in the other. You have to take a potato from a pole, then gallop back to the other end of the ring, and throw the potato into a bucket. The fastest pony does not necessarily win; you lose a lot of time if you miss the bucket because you will have to get off, remount, and try again.

You have to get four or five potatoes into the bucket, and the first one to finish is the winner.

The **egg and spoon race** is another popular gymkhana race. The rider carries a wooden spoon in one hand, with a potato (not an egg) balanced on it. The winner is usually the one with the calmest pony.

In **apple bobbing** the contestants gallop to a line of buckets with apples in the water. The riders dismount, and each rider attempts to pick up an apple with their teeth, without using their hands. When an apple has been retrieved from the bucket, the rider remounts, and gallops back to the other end of the arena. This contest usually involves getting drenched down to the shoulders.

Ride and Run is a good game as a start. It is simple; you just gallop to the end of the area, dismount and run back, leading your pony.

Musical sacks is similar to musical chairs played at parties. You need to work this game out and look ahead to see that you always have a sack between you and the next rider. You will have to control your pony, cantering slowly up to the sack and then galloping quickly to the next sack in case the music stops. Some competitors ride without stirrups to ensure that they can dismount quicker, but make sure you are in control before you try this.

Fancy Dresses Classes

There is great fun for all the family. Fancy dress classes encourage children to enter a class at a horse show and usually everyone gets a rosette. Ideas can be simple; there is no need to go for anything elaborate or expensive.

My daughter started her showing in the fancy dress class. She wore a little nurse's uniform and led her pony dressed up with bandages covered in tomato ketchup.

Make sure your pony is not alarmed by the decorations with which you adorn it. I have seen a Gretna Green pony take off in a panic around the ring, causing the bride and groom to fall off.

15 My Way

What about some advice from a teenager who has enjoyed riding with five ponies since she was eight? Georgina, aged fourteen, Marilyn Clayton's daughter, looks back on her own riding experiences.

Four out of the five ponies Georgina looked after and rode were loaned. Honey was borrowed for summer holidays; Minto was made available for holidays and half terms from Georgina's riding instructress who gave invaluable help with great patience and skill in improving Georgina's riding; Mini, a 12.2 hh. Welsh Section B, was borrowed for eighteen months from Georgina's godmother; Huckleberry, 14.2 hh. and a superb jumping pony, was loaned for three years by friends who had outgrown him; and currently Georgina has Piccadilly, a 15.2 hh. mare, purchased to enable Georgina to make the transition from pony to horse.

All the ponies were experienced, having been ridden with success by other children; they had good temperaments, and each played a part in helping Georgina to progress.

Making the change from one pony to the next is often difficult. It is so much easier if the ponies are mature and thoroughly experienced in coping with the tasks which the young rider is trying to give them. Huckleberry, for example, is inclined to take a hold and get a little excited, but he is an extremely safe, competent jumper, and Georgina learned to ride him well, winning many prizes in pony show jumping, working hunter and hunter trial competitions.

Georgina looks back on the fun, and the problems:

Honey was a small, brown, cross-bred mare, about 12 hh. She was aged over twenty; she had a sweet temperament, and was an ideal ride for me when I was eight years old. From the start she did not frighten me; we got on really well. I thoroughly enjoyed riding her. That's just the sort of pony you want at the start.

I had already basically learned to ride, but I had a lot more to discover. If Honey had frightened me it could have put me off riding for good.

She was very quiet to tack up and groom, and I learned to do this myself. I took her to my first show where we rode in the 12.2 hh. and under 'first ridden' class, and we came second. I remember that I was very worried because I had to ride her round in a little show on my own – walk, trot and canter in circles – but the judge explained exactly what to do. Honey behaved beautifully and I moved up the line ahead of other ponies who did not behave so well. I was thrilled when we were eventually placed second.

Mummy led Honey in some gymkhana classes, but then I got more confidence and rode on my own, even getting a rosette for clear round jumping over a tiny course. I fell off in the first round, but then I had another go and got a rosette for going clear at the second attempt.

Minto was a cream coloured 12.3 hh. Welsh-cross gelding. I had learned to ride on Minto at the local riding school, and was so lucky to be able to borrow him later.

He was a very experienced Pony Club competitor, and had won lots of prizes. What a clever pony. He knew all about bringing home the rosettes. He never pulled and I was always being told off for having 'washing line reins'.

Georgina with Minto. '. . . a brilliant pony, and he would always do what I wanted.'

He tended to jump quite big, so it took me a long time to get used to him jumping. I got jumped off once or twice.

Minto was a brilliant pony, and he would always

do what I wanted. He was the first pony I took hunting. I was only eight, and the first time Mummy walked, leading me, but the next time I was off a leading rein, accompanied by Mummy on a horse.

I jumped a few little rails, with Mummy giving me a lead. And it was all great fun. We didn't stay out all day; it's much better to stay out just long enough to enjoy yourself, so that you do not get too tired before you come home.

I had terrible butterflies in the stomach before going to my first hunter trial where I rode Minto in the nine and under novice and open classes. It was run by the Portman Pony Club in Dorset. I was quite worried when we walked the course, mainly because I did not think I would remember the way, but it was much easier than I thought.

Minto went round very carefully; I really enjoyed myself, and finished second in the novice, and first in the open. Mummy told me to steer for the middle of the fences, which I tried to do, and Minto did the rest. I was also told to trot between some of the fences, and as Minto had a lovely high head carriage there was not much risk of me falling over his head over the downhill fences.

Mini, short for Minstrel Boy, did frighten me a little at the start. He was a typical Welsh pony, smaller than Minto, but he pulled, which was something which was new to me, and he could show that he had a mind of his own. So I had to ride him much more firmly, with my hands and legs – all good educational stuff.

Fortunately he moved very well, and was fast which was a great help in competitions. We won a number of 12.2 hh. and under jumping classes because he was so fast when jumping against the clock. I rode him in a Kimblewick which was a big help in holding and steering him.

He was a very good hunter, and could keep up with the horses. It was on Mini that I jumped my

YOUR PONY

At home with Mini. '... he had a mind of his own.'

first hedge; not a very big one, but it was a great thrill. I used to enter him in Pony Club events and horse show classes. I learned to be very careful because he was inclined to whizz from the ring back into the collecting ring at the wrong moment. All ponies and horses jump better in the line of fences going back towards the collecting ring, but it is very embarrassing if you let them cart you out of the ring instead of finishing your round.

He was especially naughty on wet days when the reins were slippery. Once I thought I was doing a clear round, and I was about to jump the last fence, but Mini had other ideas. He ran out, causing me to fall off, dashed into the collecting ring, then galloped to the horse box area, stopping only when he got to our trailer. He was mad for food and was probably hoping this was a good way of getting his head into a bucket yet again.

When I was eleven my legs were too long for Mini; my toes began to hit the tops of the Hunt fences. I was lucky to be able to ride Huckleberry next. He was a very keen competition pony. My mother had known him for some years and always liked him; she asked for first refusal to buy him, but the owner said they would never sell him, although we could borrow him instead.

My biggest worry when I first saw him was simply that he was another grey. Mini had been so difficult to get clean that I would have loved a pony any other colour but grey! When I first rode him, at the owner's farm, I felt very nervous.

He was much bigger than I was used to; he had a long stride, and he was fit and clipped out after a season's hunting. Thank heavens, he looked after me very well when I tried to jump some of the rails and ditches on the farm.

When we got him home we found he was very keen, and he had been used to being ridden by boys who had outgrown him. They were obviously much stronger and heavier than me, and I was worried about being able to ride him properly.

Mummy decided that I should only walk and trot Huckleberry to begin with, and as the spring was approaching we turned him out with a New Zealand rug on. He soon calmed down and got fat out at grass, and was rather lazy compared with his normal behaviour. Mummy rode him while I was at school.

All this helped to make Huckleberry much more manageable by the time my school holidays came round again. When we first had him he was inclined to fizz up and canter the moment he got on to grass.

I took him to a show for the first time, and Mummy thought it would be a good idea to enter the 'Best Turned Out' class, just to see if I could control him at a show, as you only have to walk and trot round. Huckleberry behaved very well, and as he is a smart pony with a lot of presence, he won. I was very thrilled.

Huckleberry with Georgina, aged twelve, at the start of the Cottesmore Pony Club One Day Event in Leicestershire. Huckleberry is a good example of a bold, competent pony who gives confidence to the rider. He is being ridden in a Kimblewick bit and a running martingale.

He came third in the working hunter ponies, but we decided he was too keen to enter the show jumping classes at that show. All this meant that I did not try to do too much with him until I was sure I could manage him. I would advise others to do the same with a new pony. If you try to do too much straight away you can have nasty experiences. It is best to work up gradually to bigger competitions when you know your new pony really well.

I took Huckleberry to Pony Club camp, having been there before with Mini and Minto. It was at the camp that I got to know Huckleberry well. Riding him every day in lots of competitions, and instruction, with other ponies was a great help. By the time camp was over we were going together so much better.

After that we went on to win a lot of competitions in show jumping, hunter trialling, and Pony Club eventing. But sadly, after three years I outgrew him. I was so sad to give Huckleberry up. He only had one fault: he was so difficult to catch when out at grass, but he taught me to have patience in trying to do so. He was a marvellously bold pony; such fun to ride, and I was sure I would never find another pony to match him.

We tried a new pony which was very smart, but he was also much too sharp, and I simply did not get on with him. Sometimes he would put in a very definite stop at a fence, and I just could not cope with this. I had a heavy fall the first time this occurred.

Then we were lucky enough to find Piccadilly. At 15.2 hh. she seemed very big to me, and she was a very different ride to Huckleberry. She took longer to get fit, and was inclined to puff a lot, carrying a lot of weight when she had been out at grass in the summer.

I was a bit disappointed with her at first. Then I took her to our first show. Piccadilly, a brown mare aged fourteen, had shown me that she could jump at home, but she needed far more riding at a fence than Huckleberry. Plenty of leg seemed to be necessary for Dilly.

At the show I took her first into the working hunter class, and was put at the bottom of the line. The judge did not seem to think much of this ageing pony, with a few lumps and bumps on her legs, ridden by a young girl in jodphur boots, while everyone else in the class was much older, and wearing proper riding boots.

Next I took her into the novice show jumping class. At the very first fence she gave a little skip in the air, then set off in a very determined manner. She seemed absolutely at home in the ring. To my amazement we had a clear round; and in a jump off against much bigger horses, Dilly zoomed to win against the clock.

So I took her into the open show jumping class. The bigger fences seemed to suit her even better. I kicked her and she charged round, collecting herself to jump each fence carefully, winning against the clock with her first round. I came home with lots of rosettes, a silver cup and a shield, and with the

Full of resolution, Georgina and Piccadilly taking a downhill fence in hunter trials at Ketton near Stamford, Lincolnshire. Note that the rider is looking ahead and not down at the landing.

knowledge that I had a small horse who seemed to know a lot more about show jumping than I had guessed.

After that I took her into hunter trials and again she surprised me with her performances, although it was a bit more necessary to set her alight in order to finish inside the time. It is well worth finding a pony of Dilly's age, with some real experience behind it, because it does give you a great chance to enjoy yourself without worrying about teaching the pony to do its job.

I get no time for riding during term time, and it is marvellous to be able to compete on such an experienced pony when the holidays come around. She needs little or no schooling.

It is not a problem that Dilly has not so many years ahead of her as a young horse. My legs are growing fast, and I am afraid it won't be too long before I'm looking for a bigger mount – yet again.

Caring For a Pony

If I am honest I must admit to enjoying riding best of all.

I always like to think of my pony as being well looked after, happy and healthy. It can be upsetting to think of your pony outside in all weathers when you are at home cosily in front of the fire. I used to worry about this when I was younger, but I understand it more now. We always fed the ponies out at grass in the winter, and brought in the older ones at night.

My favourite of all the pony tasks is grooming. It is lovely to be close to a pony, and to talk to him at the same time as brushing and cleaning him. It is not as tiring as some of the other jobs. Grooming is best the day before a show when I am trying to make my pony look his very best. I love shampooing my pony in the summer. Mini and Huckleberry were both grey, so I had to shampoo them often, sometimes just to remove grass stains.

I am only just beginning to pull manes and tails properly. I have found it difficult; my fingers always seem to get sore. I can plait, but have only done so for the last couple of years. It was much easier than I thought. My mother always plaited my pony for me, while I put on the tail bandage and oiled the hooves. Then one day on the morning of a show the ramp of the horse box fell on my mother's head, and she had to go to hospital. We decided I should go on to the show with my friends, so there was only one thing for me to do: plait the mane myself.

Tack cleaning can be a chore, but it is important to do it thoroughly before a show or Pony Club where it might be inspected. I find it takes ages the day before a show to get everything ready: nearly the whole day is taken up with exercising, then cleaning my pony and the tack, and organizing my riding clothes.

I try to clean my tack at the end of the holidays,

and I make sure nothing needs repairing or stitching. It can be expensive and dangerous if it is left, and my mother is strict about this.

I like making quite sure my pony is in good condition. You have to watch out for different things with different ponies. With my smaller ponies we always had to guard against laminitis, and make sure they did not get too fat. I have also learned by experience to keep looking at my pony's shoes. It can be disastrous if a shoe suddenly becomes loose the day before a show, and it might stop you going.

I really regret going to a hunter trial with Dilly recently and competing in the timed section. She was jarred up afterwards, and had to be rested. It was terrible to see her like this. I never had to worry about this with my smaller ponies as their legs were so sound.

Once, when I went to check my pony turned out in the field, I noticed a friend's horse was choking. The owner called the vet who said it had eaten some dried sugar beet put out for the cattle. The sugar beet had not previously been soaked in water, so it became swollen in the horse's throat causing it to choke. It was lucky the obstruction could be removed.

At Pony Club camp you are taught to look after your pony and equipment. If you do all this normally then it is not such a shock. There are constant inspections, and the Pony Club has a high standard.

I find stable work tiring. When I was about eight or nine, I started by sweeping the yard and filling the water buckets. I can remember mucking out being exhausting at that age. I always tried to muck out before breakfast and I used to think about breakfast while doing it. It was lovely at breakfast to know I had not got it still to do. Hay and straw bales were too heavy for me to lift until the last two or three years. Before, I used to make lots of trips to the hay barn trailing hay over the yard which I then had to sweep up.

Having a pony is fun. It is lovely to care for and ride a living animal. My ponies have always been good friends. I have loved them dearly and I still see them because I know where they are. You cannot do more than your best for them, and hope they will do their best for you.

Appendix A: The Pony Club

One of the best ways to learn about riding and looking after your pony is by joining your local branch of the Pony Club. Founded in England in 1928, the Pony Club is now a worldwide youth organization open to anyone under the age of twenty-one. The organization is dedicated to guiding and encouraging young riders and is recognized for its high standard of instruction. It offers a variety of activities, including instructional rallies, lectures, mounted games, gymkhanas and Summer Camps. Whatever your standard, the Pony Club offers you the opportunity to mix with people of your age or level of experience and to compete with them on equal terms. You do not need to own your own pony to join the Pony Club; indeed, it may provide you with the opportunity to borrow a pony. It is a wonderful way of improving your riding skills whilst having immense fun and enjoyment.

To join the Pony Club you should write to the Pony Club Headquarters at the address below, giving your full name and address and the area where you ride, and enclosing a stamped-addressed envelope. You will receive details of your local branch, the names and addresses of your local District Commissioner and Secretary, and a joining form. Once your application has been processed you will receive the local branch programme.

APPENDICES

The Pony Club Headquarters
British Equestrian Centre
Stoneleigh
Kenilworth
Warwickshire CV8 2LR

Tel: 0203 696697
Fax: 0203 692351

Appendix B: Useful Addresses

British Equestrian Federation, British Equestrian Centre, Stoneleigh, Kenilworth, Warwickshire CV8 2LR.
Tel: 0203 696697   Fax: 0203 696685

British Horse Society, British Equestrian Centre, Stoneleigh, Kenilworth, Warwickshire CV8 2LR.
Tel: 0203 696697   Fax: 0203 692351

The British Show Jumping Association, British Equestrian Centre, Stoneleigh, Kenilworth, Warwickshire CV8 2LR.
Tel: 0203 696697   Fax: 0203 696685

The following disciplines/sections are also based at Stoneleigh:
Administration
Dressage
Horse and Pony Breeds
Horse Driving Trials
Horse Trials
Long Distance Riding
Road Safety
Welfare
Bridleways and Access
Riding Clubs

APPENDICES

Association of British Riding Schools, The Secretary, Old Brewery Yard, Penzance, Cornwall TR18 2SL.

British Appaloosa Society, M. Hawkins, c/o Frederick Street, Rugby CV1 2EN. Tel: 0788 860535

British Caspian Society, Rose Cottage, Clent, Nr Stourbridge, West Midlands. Tel: 0562 730483

British Palomino Society, Penrhiwllan, Llandysul, Dyfed SA44 5NZ. Tel: 0239 75387.

British Show Hack, Cob and Riding Horse Association, Rookwood, Packington Park, Meriden, Warwickshire CV7 7HF. Tel: 0676 23535.

British Show Pony Society, Mrs J. Toynton, 124 Green End Road, Sawtry, Huntingdon, Cambridgeshire. Tel: 0487 831376.

British Spotted Pony Society, Miss L. Marshall, 17 School Lane, Dronfield, Sheffield S18 6RY. Tel: 0246 413201.

Connemara Pony Breeders Society, Mrs P. Macdermott, 73 Dalysfort Road, Salthill, Galway, Ireland. Tel: 010 353 91 22909.

Dales Pony Society, Miss P. A. Fitzgerald, 196 Springvale Road, Walkely, Sheffield S6 3NU. Tel: 0742 683992.

Dartmoor Pony Society, Mrs M. Danford, Fordans, 17 Clare Court, Newbiggen Street, Thaxted, Essex CM6 2RN. Tel: 0371 830718.

Endurance Horse and Pony Society of Great Britain, Pat Payne, 22 Thornhill, Nr Wootton Bassett, Wiltshire SN4 7RX.

English Connemara Pony Society, Mrs M. V. Newman, 2 The Leys, Salford, Chipping Norton, Oxfordshire OX7 5FD. Tel: 0608 3309.

Exmoor Pony Society, D. Mansell, Glen Fern, Waddicomb, Dulverton, Somerset TA22 9RY. Tel: 0398 4490.

Fell Pony Society, Mr C. Richardson, 19 Dragley Beck, Ulverston, Cumbria LA12 0HD. Tel: 0229 52742.

Haflinger Society of Great Britain, Mrs Helen Robbins, 13 Parkfield, Pucklechurch, Bristol BS17 3NR. Tel: 0275 823479.

Highland Pony Society, I. Brown, Orwell House, Milnathort, Kinross-shire KY13 7YQ. Tel: 027 582 3479.

New Forest Pony Breeding and Cattle Society, Miss D. Macnair, Beacon Cottage, Burley, Ringwood, Hampshire BH24 4EW. Tel: 0425 32272.

Ponies Association (UK), Mrs M. Mills, 56 Green End Road, Sawtry, Huntingdon, Cambridgeshire PE17 5UY. Tel: 0487 830278.

Riding for the Disabled Association, The Secretary, Avenue R, National Agricultural Centre, Stoneleigh, Kenilworth, Warwickshire CV8 2LY. Tel: 0203 696510.

Shetland Pony Stud-Book Society, Mrs McDonald, Pedigree House, 6 King's Place, Perth PH2 8AD. Tel: 0738 23471.

Side Saddle Association, Mrs Maureen James, Highbury House, Wellford, Northampton NN6 7HT. Tel: 0858 575300.

Welsh Pony and Cob Society, J. Pritchard, 6 Chalybeate Street, Aberystwyth, Dyfed SY23 1HS. Tel: 0970 617501.

Index

advanced riding 131
age 5–6, 16–17
aids 128–9
   artificial 129
   hands 129
   legs 129
   weight 128
   voice 129
Anglo Arab 20
anti-sweat sheet 100
   see also sweat sheet
Appaloosa 17
apples 62
Arab 4, **8**, 20, 21–2, **22**

bandaging
   a pony's leg 122–3, **122–3**
   a pony's tail **75–6**, 77
barley **60**, 61–2
bay 17
behaviour problems 6–8, 36, 37, 39–40
black 17
blue roan 18
bits 88–92, **90**
body
   brush, 70, 73–4
   protector 103
boots
   brushing 101
   riding 104–5
bran 60–1, **60**
   poultice 61
brand marks 18

breathing 112
breeds 4, 5, 20–33, **24**
bridle 88–91, **89**
   assembling 90
   cleaning 97
British Show Jumping Association 196
British Show Pony Society 201
broken knees 114
brown 18
bruised soles 117
brushing 14, 115–16
bucking 40

canter 130
   advanced 134–5, **135**
   counter 135
   disunited 136
capped hocks 14, 116
carrots 62
catching a pony 6–8, 68
cavallettis 150–1
chaff **60**
chestnut 18
choosing a pony 34–45
clipping 82–3
   types of 82–3
clothing for rider 102–7
   reflective 149
coarse feed **60**, 61
colours 17–18
conformation 9–15
   head 12
   front 13

222

INDEX

forelegs 13
hind legs 13–14
middle 14
quarters 15
feet 15
Connemara **11**, 25, **25**
corns 117
coughing 112
cow hocks 14
cracked heels 118
crib biting 37
cross country 170–83
    colours 107
    fences 176–79, **176**, **177**, **178**, **179**, **180–1**
curbs 14, 115
curry comb 70, **71**, 73

Dale pony 26
dandy brush 70, **71**, 72
Dartmoor pony **23**, 26–7, **27**
day rug 100
dishing 14
dismounting 127–28, **127**
donkeys 51
dressage 183–5
dun 18

equine influenza 112, 120
    vaccination 3, 120
Exmoor pony **12**, 27–28, **28**

feed 58–65
    types of 58–62, **60**
    storage 62
feeding, programme for 63–5
fencing 49–50
Fell pony 28
first ridden pony 19
foot
    care of 2, 81
    conformation 15
    parts of 78–81, **79**
foreleg
    conformation 13
    parts of **115**

freeze brands 19

gallop 131
    advanced 136–7
Galvayne's groove 16
gloves 107
grass 58–9
    out at 2, 3, 46–7, 48–52, **98–99**
grey 18
grooming 69–77, **73–4**
    kit 70–1, **71**
gymkhana
    events 201
    pony 19

hacking jacket 105
halting 130
hats, riding 102
hay 59
head collar 66–7, 68
health 108–23
Highland pony 29
hoof *see also* foot
    brush 70, **71**, 77
    oil 70, 77
    pick 70, 71–2, **71**
Horse and Hound 35, 149
horsehage 59
hunter trials 170–82
    preparation for 170–3
    arriving at 174–5
    preparing to ride at 175
    riding the course 175–80
hunting 158–169, **164**
    autumn 160–7
    ethics 160
    tie 106, **106**
    season 167

insurance 44–5, 149

jodhpurs 103–4
jodhpur boots 104
jumping 150–7, **151**
    higher fences 153–4, **154–5**
    problems 154–7

jumping problems (continued)
    refusing 154–6
    running out 156
        hitting the fence 156–7
    stirrup length 152–3
    using kneckstrap 157
jute rug 99

keeping a pony 1–3, 46–57

lameness 113–19
laminitis 15, 47, 110
leading rein pony 19
lice 111
linseed 62
livery yards 52–3
long reining 143–5, **144**
loose box *see* stabling
lungeing 140–3, **141**

mane comb 70, **71**
mange 111
markings 18
martingales 92–3
measuring a pony 4
medicine cupboard 119–20
mounting 125–7, **125–6**
mucking out 55–7
mud fever 118

napping 39
navicular disease 116–17
New Forest pony 29–31, **30**
New Zealand rug 97–9, **98–9**
noseband 92
nostrils
    discharge from 112
    bleeding from 113

oats 60, **60**
oiling a pony's feet 76, **77**
on the bit 137–38
overreach 114–15

Palomino 18, 22–3
pedal ostitis 117

Piebald 18
pigeon toes 14
plaiting 14
plaiting a mane 194–6, **195**
points of the horse 17, **17**
poll guard 101
polo pony 20
pony, types of 19–21
Pony Club, the 2, 106, 145, 149, 158, 159, 164, **164**, 165, 172, **182**, *see also* Appendix A
    camp 145
    eventer 20
    eventing **182**, 183–5
    rallies 69, 145
pony nuts 61, **61**
pony trekking 29
pulse, pony's 122

quick release knot 67–68, **67**

rearing 39
rein back 137
riding a pony 124–45
riding mac 107
ringbones 117
ringworm 111
roads and roadsense 2, 6, 40, 146–49
rubber curry comb 70, **71**
rugs 97–101
    cleaning 100–2

saddle
    parts of 85–6, **85**
    position in 128
saddles 84–7, 93, 96
saddlery 84–101
    looking after 93–4
    cleaning 94–7
safety stirrups 88
sandcrack 118
salt lick 62
schooling a pony 131–45
seat 138–40
seedy toe 118

INDEX

sesamoiditis 117
sexes 16
Shetland pony 30
shoeing 2, 78
show hunter pony 20, **189**, **190**
show jumping 196–7
   clear round 198
   penalties 197
show jumping pony 20
show pony **10**, 20
showing 186–201
   classes 198–199
   handy pony class 198
   preparation for 188–96
   working pony 199–201, **200**
sidebones 117
skewbald 18
skin disorders 111
snaffles 91–2
spavin 116
   test 44
splints 14
sponges 70
sponsored rides 182
sprains 114
strawberry roan 18
stable rubber or cloth 70, 75
stables and stabling 2, 3, 46–7, 52–7, 55
straw 60
studs 81
stirrup leathers and irons 87
summer sheet 100
sweat scraper 70, **71**
sweat sheet 77
   see also anti-sweat sheet
sweet itch 111
swellings 111–12

tack *see* saddlery
   cleaning 94–7

tail bandage 70, **71**
   tying a **75**–**6**, 77
tail guard 101
teeth 16, 121
temperament 4, 5, 6–9
temperature, pony's 121
   taking a 121
tetanus 3, 120
   vaccination 121
Thoroughbred 4, 16, 20–1, **21**
thoroughpins 116
thrush 118–119
transporting a pony 172–3, **173**
trimming 191–4
   mane 192–3
   tails 193
   extra 193–4
   feet 2
trot 130
   advanced **133**, 133–4
   extended 134
turning 129

vaccinations 3, 121
vetting a pony 42–4

walk 129
   advanced 132–3, **132**
washing a pony 77–78
water 50–1
water brush 70, **71**, 75
weaving 37
Welsh pony 31, **32**
whips 107
windgalls 116
windsucking 37
wisp 70
working hunter pony 20, **171**, **190**, **200**
worms and worming 2, 110–11

225